Flavor

without

Fat

Cookbook for Healthy Living for the Entire Family

By Jan McBarron, M.D.

Third Edition, 1997

ISBN 0-9622923-3-8

Published by

Quill Publications, Inc.
Columbus, Georgia 31908

A Special Thanks

This book is a result of hours of hard work in researching, testing, and sampling hundreds of recipes. My deepest gratitude is extended to all my patients, staff, friends, my mother, and my husband, Duke.

Table of Contents

Nutrition Information

Recipes

To everyone in search of better health and an improved quality of life.

CHAPTER ONE

A Closer Look

When I was over 200 pounds, I counted calories in a desperate attempt to control my weight. Now I wear a size seven and I count fat instead of calories. It's easier, I eat at least three times a day, and I am seldom hungry.

A high carbohydrate, moderate protein, low fat diet is the easiest and healthiest of all diets. It is an excellent diet, not only for women, but for men and children over six as well. Of course, it's advisable to check with your doctor before starting any diet, but eating a low fat diet is always preferable to a high fat diet. The American Heart Association and the National Institute of Health advocate a low fat diet.

A diet consisting of less than 30% and ideally less than 20% fat is considered a low fat diet. This means a person's total caloric intake for the day should have no more than 30% of its calories from fat. Currently, most Americans consume a 40% – 60% fat diet.

The New England Journal of Medicine recently reported that in the past 20 years red meat consumption had fallen by 38.8%, butter by 33.3%, and whole milk and cream by 24.1%. In practical terms, this means that Americans who used to drink 110 quarts of whole milk each year, which was the national average, are now consuming just 50 quarts. And it is paying off. Although heart disease is still epidemic, since 1978 the number of people dying from heart disease in the United States has dropped by 29%.

At first glance, this seems like a tremendous step forward. However, a closer look at the entire dietary pattern is alarming. A USDA analysis reveals that the intake of certain fatty foods has decreased while the intake of other fatty foods is on the rise. In other words, one set of high fat foods has been exchanged for another set.

BEEF

Each of us still eats over 60 pounds of beef annually.

Males have continued to eat red meat, listing steaks, hot dogs, and hamburgers as their most frequently consumed foods. Females, on the other hand, get their fat from margarine, dairy foods, mayonnaise, and salad dressing.

PORK

The consumption of pork has remained steady over the past 19 years at about 45 pounds per person annually.

POULTRY

Poultry has been gaining steadily in consumption, but again the figures are misleading. Although Americans eat chicken twice as often today as in 1970, cooking methods transform it from a low fat food to a high fat food: fried chicken, greasy fast food nuggets, chicken hot dogs, frozen entrées in fat rich sauces. The same basic problem exists with turkey.

DAIRY

In the consumption of dairy products there is a sharp decrease in whole milk and an equally sharp increase in "low fat 2%" milk. Ice cream consumption has remained steady at about 18 gallons per person per year. Since 1968, the consumption of high fat, hard cheese has more than doubled to about 22 pounds per person per year.

Consumption of butter and lard is lower, but we are eating more salad oils and cooking oils, about 27 pounds per person per year. Margarine has stayed at about 10 pounds per year. A four-inch croissant can contain as much as four teaspoons of butter! One plain 3.5-ounce doughnut is about 50% fat and contains as many calories as four slices of bread with jam.

GRAINS

Americans are now eating about 17% more fiber foods. We still eat less than the amount of bread, cereal, pasta, and rice that our grandparents did in 1910.

CHAPTER TWO

Food Groups

Foods are classified into three groups: Carbohydrate, Protein and Fat. Although many foods are a combination of two or three groups, foods are categorized by their highest content. For example, beans are a source of all three groups but contain more protein than carbohydrate and fat, so these are considered a protein.

CARBOHYDRATE

Carbohydrates can be divided into two types: *simple* and *complex.*

Complex: These foods take a considerable amount of time to digest and raise blood sugar slowly. They are an excellent energy source. There are four calories to a gram of carbohydrate. Examples include potatoes, rice, pasta, and breads.

Simple: These foods raise blood sugar rapidly, within minutes. Generally, within a few hours the blood sugar drops drastically, producing a multitude of symptoms including nausea, sweating, jitters, irritability, fatigue, lack of concentration, and strong cravings for sweets. These also yield four calories to a gram. Examples include sugar, candy, and icing.

PROTEIN

Protein foods contain nitrogen. This means work for the liver to process the nitrogen and the kidney to excrete it. Protein is needed to maintain muscle tissue for growth and some metabolic functions. Americans have a love affair with protein and for the most part consume far too much. Of interest, if a person is on a weight loss diet that is too high in protein and too low in complex carbohydrate he often suffers from irritability, fatigue, and depression.

Protein yields four calories to one gram. Protein foods include meat, cheese, fish, eggs, and beans.

PROTEIN: More is not better!

Asked to identify the most important component of a healthy diet, most people would answer, "Protein." There is a foundation for this belief, since protein is required throughout life to maintain and build body tissues, form antibodies, make hemoglobin in the blood, and produce important enzymes and hormones. Unfortunately, the amount needed to be eaten each day has been overestimated. Important as it is as a nutritional "building block," protein is not required in abundance. The Recommended Daily Allowance (RDA) for protein is shown in Chart A.

CHART A

Population	Age	Grams of Protein
Children	1-3	23
	4-6	30
	7-10	34
Males	11-14	45
	15+	56
Females*	11-18	45
	19+	44

*Pregnant females should add 30 grams to the figure given for their age group; breast-feeding women should add 20 grams.

For an adult, the RDA is no more than 0.8 grams of protein per kilogram (2.2 pounds) of body weight, or about 56 grams for an average size man and 45 grams for an average size woman. (Athletes need about 1.2 grams per kilogram of weight.) To put this in perspective, 56 grams of protein are provided by a meal containing four ounces of white meat turkey, two slices of whole wheat bread, an eight-ounce glass of skim milk, and a banana.

Far more protein is consumed in the United States than is needed for good nutrition. There has been a steady trend away from low fat vegetable protein and toward high fat animal protein. Today, about 70% of protein consumed comes from animal meat and dairy products.

Nutritionalists believe the proper ratio to be just the opposite: about one-third from animals and two-thirds from plants.

While red meat is rich in protein, it is an even richer source of undesirable fat. Luncheon meats and sausages are fun foods, tasty and easy to eat, and they do contain protein. Unfortunately, they're loaded with fat (as well as sodium and, in many instances, dangerous additives).

Fortunately, a number of low fat sources of protein do exist. Small pieces of fish, skinless poultry, and extra lean beef added as a condiment to pasta, rice, or vegetables can contribute valuable protein. So can beans and legumes, which can be added to soups, rice, and salads. Skim and low fat diary foods are also excellent sources of protein.

FAT

There are two kinds of fat: *saturated* and *unsaturated*. The difference is in the molecular structure of the fat, and also in the way they affect your body.

Saturated fats are generally solid at room temperature, and of animal origin. Examples include meat, poultry, fish, and dairy products. The only plant sources of saturated fat include palm, coconut, and palm kernel oil. Too much saturated fat in your diet can lead to heart disease because the fat does not easily break down in your bloodstream, and tends to build up on your blood vessel walls. That can cause circulation problems, strokes, and heart disease.

Unsaturated fats are generally liquid at room temperature and are of plant origin. These include two types:

polyunsaturated and monounsaturated. Both are more healthful because they lower cholesterol in the blood and provide a certain degree of coronary (heart) protection. Polyunsaturated fats include safflower, soybean, sunflower, corn, cotton seed, and sesame oils. Monounsaturated oils include olive, canola, peanut, avocado, and nut oils.

To maintain weight and lead a healthier life, you must limit the fat in your diet. Remember, carbohydrates and proteins contain four calories per gram. Fats, however, contain nine calories per gram. That's why fat is often called *dense, calorie laden,* or *concentrated.*

FLAVOR WITHOUT FAT

CHAPTER THREE

Fat in Detail

FAT BEGETS FAT

Not all food calls for the same amount of energy in the conversion process, so not all have the same "handling cost." Research conducted by Dr. Jean-Pierre Flatt of the University of Massachusetts Medical School indicates that almost one-fourth (23%) of the calories found in carbohydrates are burned off when they are converted to fat. So, of 100 calories processed, only 77% are available to be stored as body fat. But dietary fat uses just three calories in energy to process 100 calories into body fat. This means 97% of all fat calories are converted to body fat. Fat is more fattening, calorie for calorie, than carbohydrates.

AMERICANS EAT TO DIE

The impact of the modern diet on health is the subject of the *1988 Surgeon General's Report on Nutrition and Health*. The report, which paints a picture of the United States gobbling its way to the grave, found a causal link between a high fat diet and the five leading causes of death.

The fact is, 2,000 Americans die every day, 365 days a

year, from a single cause, coronary heart disease. Outnumbering cancer and auto accidents, this disease is by far the number one killer of Americans and is rampant throughout the country. Consider the following:

- One person suffers a heart attack every minute.

- Each year there are 1.5 million heart attacks resulting in 600,000 to 800,000 deaths.

- The chance of an American dying of heart and blood vessel disease is about one out of two.

- By age 60, every fifth male in the United States has suffered a heart attack.

- Twice as many women die each year from cardiovascular disease as from all types of cancer.

In addition to heart disease, fat in our diets is closely associated with cancer. The fat/cancer link is profound.

Colon cancer: This disease is responsible for 51,000 deaths a year. Each year it is diagnosed in some 41,000 men and 29,000 women. Five years later, only about half this number are still alive.

Breast cancer: One out of every 10 women develops breast cancer. Every 13 minutes another woman dies of the disease. Despite all efforts, this is at the same rate today as in 1950.

Prostate cancer: This accounts for more than 18% of all male cancers, and is responsible for more than 25,000 deaths each year. Before 1900, prostate cancer was considered a rare disease. Today, as a result of our fatty diet, it is a major cause of cancer death in males.

Colon, breast, and prostate cancer accounted for 39% of all new cancer cases and 27% of all cancer deaths in 1988. This is an enormous price to pay for high fat eating habits.

The U.S. diet contributes to cancer risk in three ways. Dietary fat acts as a cancer promoter in cells. Dietary fat contributes to being overweight and obesity, and is an independent risk for certain cancers. Foods rich in dietary fat often replace healthier food choices, such as fresh fruits, vegetables, and whole grains.

Fat is lethal to a diet, and lethal if you want to lose weight. Knowledge about fat and how it affects your body is extremely important.

1. Gram for gram, fat has more than twice the calories as carbohydrate and protein.

2. Carbohydrate, protein, and fat all have the potential to be converted and stored as fat by your body, but fat is stored most easily.

3. The conversion and storage of fatty foods into body fat require the least amount of energy when compared to carbohydrate and protein.

It's virtually impossible (and not healthy) to go on a *fat-free* diet. Most foods are not pure. They are combinations of carbohydrate, protein, and fat.

13

WHAT IS FAT?

Fat is made up of carbon, hydrogen, and oxygen atoms. The different kinds of fat are distinguished by differences in chemical structure. The building blocks of fat are fatty acids. Fatty acids are saturated, monounsaturated, or polyunsaturated.

However, fat does help keep us healthy in several ways because it

- Provides linoleic acid, a fatty acid essential to proper growth, healthy skin, and cholesterol metabolism.

- Helps transport, absorb, and store the fat soluble vitamins A, D, E, and K.

- Insulates and cushions body organs.

- Supplies energy. It's the most concentrated source of calories with nine calories per gram of fat versus four calories per gram of protein and carbohydrate.

- Satisfies us. Because it takes longer to digest, fat stays with us longer, helping to control hunger. What's more, *it tastes good!*

Saturated fats are solid at room temperature and are found mainly in animal sources. Tropical fats—coconut, palm, and palm kernel oils—are unique because they come from plants, yet they too contain significant amounts of saturated fats. Scientific evidence demonstrates a link between a diet high in saturated fats and the incidence of high blood cholesterol.

Fats and oils that contain mainly unsaturated fatty acids are liquid at room temperature and are found most commonly in plant sources. Olive oil and peanut oil are high in monounsaturated fats, while corn, soybean, safflower, and sunflower oils contain considerable amounts of polyunsaturated fat.

With so much attention on fat in our diet, and with so many different types of fat, it could be very confusing. However, this little lesson on fat should help to clarify it. Whenever discussing fat, consider that all fat falls into one of two categories, saturated or unsaturated. Saturated fat comes from animal products with the exception of coconut, palm, and palm kernel oil. Unsaturated fat is derived from plant sources. Not all fat is bad for you. Saturated fat seems to pose the most serious health consequences and should be monitored closely. As a general rule of thumb, everyone over the age of four should have total fat in his diet less than 30%, preferably less than 20%. Of the fat in your diet, most of this should be unsaturated fat.

In the category of unsaturated fats, there are monounsaturated, polyunsaturated, omega-3, and omega-6 fats. As stated earlier, the monounsaturated fats include olive and peanut oil. Most other vegetable oils are polyunsaturated. The omega-3 fat is a type of polyunsaturated fat found predominantly in fish. As a general rule, the higher the fat content of the seafood the more omega-3 fatty acid content. Research suggests that a diet rich in omega-3 fatty acid may help reduce the risk of heart disease. Research continues on omega-6 fat but at this point these two are considered healthy fats. Examples of omega-6 fatty acids include black currant oil and evening primrose oil.

All foods that contain dietary fat are actually a mix-

15

ture of saturated and unsaturated (monounsaturated and/or polyunsaturated) fatty acids. Choose fats that contain more unsaturated fat than saturated fat. But the level of saturation of any fat can be altered by a process called hydrogenation.

Hydrogenation is a way to change unsaturated fatty acids to a saturated chemical structure. This is accomplished by adding more hydrogen to the fatty acid molecule. To increase stability or "shelf-life" some alterations such as hydrogenation of the oil is often necessary. Shortening made by blending hydrogenated vegetable oils, like coconut or palm oil, can improve flavor and extend the shelf-life of packaged foods. So be sure to watch out for these, as they are unhealthy fats.

So for a quick summary lesson on fat, remember the following: Saturated fat comes from animals that live on the land. It is also found in coconut and palm kernel. Saturated fat should be avoided. Unsaturated fat comes from plants and fish. Our diet should obtain less than 30% of its calories from fat and most of this fat should come from the unsaturated category. The American Heart Association suggests consuming no more than 10% of daily calories as saturated fat and dividing the remaining 20% of calories from fat between monounsaturated and polyunsaturated fat.

Another category of fat, called *omega-3 fatty acids*, is unique. These are highly polyunsaturated fatty acids found in fish, shellfish, and plants from the sea. As a general rule, the higher the fat content of the seafood, the more omega-3 fatty acids it contains. Research suggests that diets rich in omega-3 fatty acids may help reduce the risk of heart disease.

CHAPTER FOUR

Ideal Nutrition

Whether you want to lose weight or maintain your current size, you need a balanced mix of nutrients.

Remember, one gram of protein or one gram of carbohydrate has approximately four calories, while one gram of fat averages nine calories. Because carbohydrates are the body's most efficient source of fuel, it is best to choose carbohydrates as the dietary mainstay. Meat or protein should be a secondary choice of calories. Eliminate empty calories by decreasing sugar, fat, and alcohol whenever possible.

Regardless of whether you eat to maintain your ideal weight or to reach it, the daily percentage of calories you derive from these three sources is important. Strive to make carbohydrates (particularly complex carbohydrates) at least 50% of your diet. Protein should be approximately 20% and fat limited to 30% or less. The fat should be mostly unsaturated with only 10% saturated.

IDEAL WEIGHT

The most common measurement of ideal, or most desirable, body weight has been the Metropolitan Life Insurance Company's height and weight table. It provides a range of weight-for-height, with the midpoint considered the ideal weight for most people.

Fortunately, there is a simple formula for estimating ideal weight.

1. Measure your height.

2. For males, the first five feet is equal to 106 pounds. Each additional inch is equal to an additional six pounds.

3. For females, the first five feet is equal to 100 pounds. Each additional inch is equal to an additional five pounds.

4. Give or take 10% of this weight to determine the weight range, the lowest weight corresponding to small boned people and the highest weight to big boned people.

Ideal Weight Chart

Men Ideal Weight	Height	Women Ideal Weight
106	5'0"	100
112	5'1"	105
118	5'2"	110
124	5'3"	115
130	5'4"	120
136	5'5"	125
142	5'6"	130
148	5'7"	135
154	5'8"	140
160	5'9"	145
166	5'10"	150
172	5'11"	155
178	6'0"	160
184	6'1"	165
190	6'2"	170
196	6'3"	175
202	6'4"	180

Permanent changes in excessive body fat should take place on a slow, steady basis over a period of time, and involve three key steps.

1. Reduce dietary fat.
2. Increase high carbohydrate, high fiber foods as a low calorie means to satisfy appetite.
3. Increase exercise to burn calories, stoke metabolism, and reduce *fat tooth* cravings.

The U.S. population is carrying more than 1.5 billion pounds of excess weight. For most of us, the real problem is being *overfat*, that is, carrying too much body fat.

Remember:

- Excess body fat is a health risk, particularly for coronary heart disease, cancer, stroke, and diabetes. Know how to calculate your ideal weight. Don't rely on height/weight tables.
- Excessive dietary fat produces an "overfat" condition because dietary fat is calorically dense and is easily converted into body fat.
- Chronic dieting doesn't work. It can set you up to gain weight by diminishing metabolism and increasing *fat tooth* cravings.
- It takes a negative energy balance of 3,500 calories to lose a pound of body fat. This is accomplished by reducing caloric intake (*trimming fat from the diet*) and increasing caloric output (*exercise*).

Daily Fat Intake

Total Calories	Total Fat Calories per Day	Grams of Fat per Day	Saturated Fat Calories per Day	Grams of Saturated Fat per Day
1,000	300	33	100	11
1,200	360	40	120	13
1,400	420	46	140	15
1,600	480	53	160	18
1,800	540	60	180	20
2,000	600	66	200	22
2,200	660	73	220	24
2,400	720	80	240	26
2,600	780	86	160	29
2,800	840	93	280	31
3,000	900	100	300	33
3,200	960	106	320	35
3,400	1,020	113	340	38
3,600	1,080	120	360	40
3,800	1,140	126	380	42

FLAVOR WITHOUT FAT

CHAPTER FIVE

Percent Fat

To eat less than 30% fat in our diet, we must be able to calculate the fat percentage in foods. This is relatively easy. Read the nutritional information on the label and observe the total number of grams of fat and calories per serving. Since fat has nine calories per gram, simply multiply the number of grams by nine to learn the total fat calories. Next, divide the total fat calories by the total number of calories per serving. Convert this to percentage by using the formula in Chart A.

Chart A

Calories 190	Grams Fat 16

$$16 \times 9 = \frac{144 \text{ Fat Calories}}{190 \text{ Calories}} = .75 \text{ or } 75\%$$

And you thought peanut butter was good for you!

Since good health guidelines recommend eating less than 30% fat, a 75% fat food is not good. Remember, if you calculate the fat percentage for all your foods you will be in good shape.

Tips:

1. If each food you eat throughout the day is less than 30% fat, your entire fat total for the day will be less than 30%.

2. If a food doesn't have the nutrition information on the label, it is probably too high in fat, so skip it.

3. All fruits have less than 30% fat as do most vegetables, with the exception of avocados and olives. However, these are unsaturated fats and not really as bad as saturated (animal) fats.

4. When reading the label, use the total number of grams of fat. Sometimes a label will provide a fat breakdown.

   For example: Fat   7 gm

   Unsaturated 4 gm

   Saturated   3 gm

   Use the number 7 for this product.

5. If you really dislike math and want a quick, easy rule, then use this. For every 100 calories, the food should have no more than three grams of fat. Therefore, a 200 calorie food should have not more than six grams of fat, a 300 calorie food, nine grams of fat, and a 400 calorie food, 12 grams of fat.

CHAPTER SIX

Cholesterol

Coronary heart disease is a condition in which blood flow to the heart is restricted due to the buildup of cholesterol blockages, or plaque, on the inner walls of the coronary arteries. It is the product of a disease called atherosclerosis.

One of the most important cholesterol studies is in Framingham, Massachusetts, where investigators have continuously monitored the cardiac health of the population since 1948. Their findings are conclusive: As blood cholesterol rises, so does the incidence of heart attack. According to Dr. William Castelli, director of the Framingham study, for every 1% rise in cholesterol above 150 mg/dl, the risk of heart attack goes up by 2%.

In the appropriate amount, cholesterol is not harmful. It is necessary for cell wall construction, for the transmission of nerve impulses, and for the synthesis of important steroid and sex hormones. The higher a person's cholesterol count, the greater the risk for heart disease. And the opposite is also true. Lowering the blood cholesterol level reduces the risk for heart disease.

Table A shows the risk at different levels according to the National Institute of Health.

Cholesterol Level

Age	Moderate Risk	High Level	Excellent
20 & under	180 plus	200 plus	under 180
21-29	200 plus	220 plus	under 180
30-39	220 plus	240 plus	under 200
40 plus	240 plus	260 plus	under 200

Type of cholesterol also has an impact on cardiac risk. Low density lipoprotein, or LDL cholesterol, endangers cardiac health; high density lipoprotein, or HDL cholesterol, promotes cardiac health.

An easy way to remember the type of cholesterol is as follows: Cholesterol is a fat that cannot flow freely in the bloodstream but requires a protein (a little car) for transportation. HDL (think of "H" for happy) picks up cholesterol from around the body and carries it to the liver for removal. LDL (think of "L" for lousy) carries cholesterol from the liver and takes it out into the circulatory system, depositing it along blood vessels, causing hardening of the arteries and death.

For many hormonal reasons LDL is always higher. HDL is considered good if greater than 55 mg/dl.

There are two ways to improve the HDL ratio:

1. Increase HDLs. This can be done by losing excess weight and by giving up cigarette smoking. Also, exercise is an excellent way to increase HDLs. As few as three workouts a week for 20 minutes can improve HDL. Studies find that joggers and brisk walkers who cover just 11 miles per week have significantly higher HDLs than their sedentary counterparts.
2. Decrease LDLs. The most effective way to lower LDLs, apart from medication, is to reduce saturated fats in the diet.

WHAT IS CHOLESTEROL?

Essential to life, cholesterol is produced by the body. A soft, waxy, fat-like substance, cholesterol is found only in animal foods. Health experts recommend that we limit the dietary cholesterol to 300 milligrams each day.

Cholesterol Level of Selected Foods

FOOD	MEASURE	CHOLESTEROL
Beef	3 oz	80
Butter	1 Tbsp	35
Cheddar cheese	1 oz	30
Chicken, *dark meat* *w/o skin*	3 oz	79
Chicken, *light meat* *w/o skin*	3 oz	72
Custard pie	1 slice	120
Egg	1	274
Ice cream	1 cut	60
Lamb and veal	3 oz	83
Liver	4 oz	524
Lobster	3 1/2 oz	70
Margarine (vegetable oil)	1 Tbsp	0
Milk (whole)	8 oz	34
Milk (skim)	8 oz	4
Peanut butter	2 Tbsp	0
Pizza	1 slice	40
Pork	3 oz	76
Salmon	3 oz	69
Scallops	3 1/2 oz	36
Shrimp	3 1/2 oz	66
Snow crab	3 1/2 oz	75
Sweetbread	4 oz	560
Turkey, *dark meat* *w/o skin*	3 oz	72
Turkey, *white meat* *w/o skin*	3 oz	59
White bread	1 slice	1
Wine	3 1/2 oz	0
Yogurt	1 oz	29

If you haven't had a cholesterol check in the past year, it is a healthy idea to schedule one soon. See your physician.

TRIGLYCERIDES

Many people are confused about cholesterol and triglycerides. Triglycerides are a completely different fat molecule than cholesterol. But like cholesterol, triglycerides dissolve poorly in the blood and can cause many of the same vascular diseases—heart failure, stroke, kidney problems, and high blood pressure.

Foods high in cholesterol are often high in triglycerides also. If you eat a diet low in cholesterol, you'll probably reduce your triglyceride level at the same time. Consuming too much alcohol, a lot of fried food, and an excess of simple carbohydrates can cause your body to produce excess triglycerides. You can be tested for triglycerides at the same time you have your cholesterol checked. Your triglyceride level is generally considered high if it exceeds 150 milligrams.

Triglyceride levels can be lowered by the above mentioned dietary changes and by exercise. The same walking program that lowers cholesterol will also lower triglyceride levels.

CHAPTER SEVEN

Salt

Americans eat too much salt. It is often done unconsciously. Hidden salt is found in canned soups, cereals, cheese, snacks, hot dogs, frozen foods, soft drinks, pizza, and processed foods. The list goes on and on. All of these foods either contain salt, or are processed with salt. And that means you're taking in a lot of salt before you ever pick up that salt shaker from the table. (Using the shaker makes the problem even worse!)

What is so bad about salt? It makes blood pressure rise and that can cause a host of other problems including vascular disease, heart trouble, strokes, and kidney problems.

Compare a blood vessel to a garden hose. As blood flows through your vessels, it creates pressure on the vessel walls, just as a garden hose has pressure on it when you turn on the water.

When you eat salt, it attracts water. You may notice bloating somewhere on your body when you eat a lot of salty food—swollen feet and ankles, swollen hands, and puffy eyes. Salt actually pulls water along with it wherever it goes, and that includes in the bloodstream.

The normal flow of blood in your vessels is suddenly increased when you add salt, because water is added to the flow. Can you visualize what happens? Think of turning up the pressure on the garden hose—where more and more fluid is added.

In measuring blood pressure, we get two figures; one should always be higher than the other. The top figure, which is higher, is called systolic blood pressure. It represents the pressure on the vessel walls each time the heart pumps. The bottom figure is called the diastolic blood pressure, and it measures the pressure on the walls between heartbeats.

There's no such thing as a "normal" blood pressure for everybody, just as there's no "normal" weight for everybody. Normal is actually a range. Most physicians evaluate blood pressure over different intervals to study the trend of blood pressure to discover if there is a problem.

Blood pressure fluctuates throughout the day, depending on what you're doing, what stresses you're facing, and even what you eat. (Remember, salt raises your blood pressure.)

There are many other contributing factors to blood pressure. Some you can control; some you can't. Among these factors:

1. *Age*—The older you get, the more elevated the blood pressure.
2. *Gender*—Blood pressure problems are more common in men.
3. *Race*—Blood pressure problems are more common in blacks.
4. *Smoking*—This habit causes the blood vessels to constrict, and that increases pressure.
5. *Obesity*—The heart is trying to push blood through a greater body area and this resistance causes an increase in blood pressure.

6. *Stress, anxiety, tension*—Heart rate is elevated by the release of adrenaline, a hormone that increases blood pressure.

7. *Drugs*—Remember that any drug, prescription or illegal, is a chemical. One side effect of many of these chemicals is constriction of the blood vessels, which raises blood pressure.

8. *Alcohol*—Research has shown that alcohol has the same effect on blood vessels as any other drug—constricting vessels and raising blood pressure.

9. *Pregnancy*—During pregnancy, pressure may be higher because the total volume of blood in the body increases.

10. *Lack of exercise*—Those who don't exercise have weaker cardiovascular systems, which can lead to higher blood pressure.

11. *Salt*—Remember the analogy between blood vessels and the garden hose. Salt holds water and therefore increases blood pressure.

Age, gender, and race are uncontrollable factors. But what about your weight? What about habits such as drinking and smoking? What about lack of exercise, or eating salty foods? You can change many factors that cause high blood pressure, and perhaps salt should be first on the list.

It's not easy to give up eating salt. Salt is already added to many of the foods we eat. The first thing you can do, however, is to get rid of the shaker on your table. You don't need it. You should never add salt to your food. At first, you'll notice a difference in the taste. However, soon you'll grow to enjoy food without salt. A person acquires a taste for salt by eating it more and more often. Learning to eat food without added salt is also an acquired taste that is accomplished through repeated practice.

Next, look for ways you can eliminate salt from cooking. Many times, salt is added to recipes strictly for taste and not as a necessary ingredient. Finally, read labels carefully. If salt is one of the first three ingredients, then you'll know that item contains too much salt.

CHAPTER EIGHT

Fiber

Fiber is another advertising buzzword these days. Is there a breakfast cereal left that doesn't boast of its fiber content? Aren't we also told that fiber is good for us, that it might help prevent colon cancer and facilitate digestion?

Yes, fiber is certainly a most popular word in advertising today. And with some good reason. But be cautious. You should eat fiber, but fiber is only part of a well-balanced diet that includes all the other things discussed previously. Eating fiber alone will not solve all your weight or nutritional problems.

What is fiber? It is the part of plant material our bodies cannot digest. As fiber passes through the digestive system, it absorbs water and adds bulk to the stool, resulting in regular, healthy bowel movements (also preventing hemorrhoids and constipation).

Fiber also slows down the digestive process, which promotes better carbohydrate and insulin activity. In addition, as fiber passes through the colon, it helps scrape old cells from the inside lining of the colon. It is believed that this cleansing action helps prevent certain types of colon cancer. The theory is that fiber might help scrape away pre-cancerous cells before they cause trouble. This is still a theory and has not been proved. Several studies are underway.

However, there's no doubt that fiber is good for you. And, today, with the advent of high fiber cereals and breads, it's easy, inexpensive, and palatable to add more fiber to your diet.

If you're now eating a diet high in fiber, that's great; keep it up. If you are not, please start, but with a word of caution. You must add fiber to your diet gradually or else you may experience an increase in gas and bloating. If you have these symptoms while starting a high fiber diet, cut back on the fiber and add it gradually in small amounts each day.

Note: For people with special stomach or intestinal problems, consult your physician before increasing the fiber in your diet.

How do you increase the fiber in your diet? It's easy. Whole grain products, fruits, vegetables, and beans are all high in fiber. Also, foods that are not processed usually are high in fiber. Enjoy brown rice instead of white rice, apples with the skin instead of applesauce, and baked potatoes with the skin rather than mashed potatoes.

There are two kinds of fiber: water insoluble and water soluble. Water insoluble fiber is also known as crunchy fiber (an older term, not used much anymore, is crude fiber). It's found in foods such as breads and cereals.

Water soluble fiber is a gummy fiber found in things such as oatmeal, bran, apples, and beans. These water soluble fibers have recently been touted for their ability to help reduce cholesterol levels. Those claims are now being studied, but some evidence exists that water soluble fiber does reduce cholesterol levels.

Both types of fiber are excellent and promote health. They should be added to the diet daily.

To determine how much fiber is in a food, especially cereal, read the label. Look for the term dietary fiber. This is a combination of both water soluble and water insoluble fiber. Study the labels, not the advertising hype on the front of the package. Some cereals claim or imply they are high in fiber, but a closer examination of the label reveals only one, two, three, or four grams of fiber. Other cereals have 12 and 13 grams of fiber per serving. Naturally, select those cereals highest in dietary fiber.

The National Cancer Institute recommends eating 25 to 30 grams of fiber a day. Unfortunately, most people are lucky if they get 10 to 12 grams a day.

Fiber Content of Selected Foods

FOOD	SERVING SIZE	FIBER (GRAMS)	CALORIES
Cereals–High Fiber			
100% Bran	1/2 c (1 oz)	9.0	75
Kellogg's All Bran®	1/3 c (1 oz)	9.0	70
Fiber One®	1/3 c (1 oz)	12.0	90
Cereals–Medium Fiber			
Corn Bran®	2/3 c (1 oz)	5.0	100
Bran Chex®	2/3 c (1 oz)	5.0	90
Most®	2/3 c (1 oz)	4.0	95
Post 40% Bran Flakes®	3/4 c (1 oz)	4.0	90
Raisin Bran	3/4 c (1 oz)	4.0	115
Cereals–Low Fiber			
Honey Bran®	7/8 c (1 oz)	3.0	100
Wheat Germ	1/4 c (2 oz)	3.0	110
Total®	1 c (1 oz)	2.0	100
Wheat Chex®	2/3 c (1 oz)	2.0	100
Wheaties®	1 c (1 oz)	2.0	100
Special K®	1 1/3 c (1 oz)	2.0	100
Oatmeal	3/4 c (1 oz)	2.0	100
Cheerios®	1 1/4 c (1 oz)	1.0	110
Grape-Nuts®	1/4 c (1 oz)	1.0	100

Fiber Content of Selected Foods

FOOD	SERVING SIZE	FIBER (GRAMS)	CALORIES
Breads			
Crisp bread, rye	2 crackers	2.0	50
Crisp bread, wheat	2 crackers	2.0	50
Whole wheat bread	1 slice	1.4	60
Pumpernickel bread	1 slice	1.0	70
Cracked wheat	1 slice	1.0	60
Mixed grain	1 slice	0.9	60
French bread	1 slice (1 1/2 oz)	0.7	100
Bagel, plain	1 bagel (1 oz)	0.6	150
Oatmeal	1 slice	0.5	60
Pita bread (5")	1 piece	0.4	120
White bread	1 slice	0.4	80
Fruits			
Apple (w/skin)	1 med	3.5	80
Pear (w/skin)	1/2 large	3.1	60
Raisins	1/4 c	3.1	110
Raspberries	1/2 c	3.1	35
Strawberries	1 c	3.0	45
Prunes	3	3.0	60
Apple (w/o skin)	1 med	2.7	70
Orange	1	2.6	60
Pear (w/o skin)	1/2 large	2.5	60
Banana	1 med	2.4	105

Fiber Content of Selected Foods

FOOD	SERVING SIZE	FIBER (GRAMS)	CALORIES
Blueberries	1/2 c	2.0	40
Dates	3	1.9	70
Peach (w/skin)	1	1.9	40
Apricots (fresh)	3 med	1.8	50
Grapefruit	1/2	1.6	40
Apricots (dried)	5 halves	1.4	40
Peach (w/o skin)	1	1.2	40
Cherries, sweet	10	1.2	50
Pineapple	1/2 c	1.1	40
Cantaloupe	1/4 melon	1.0	30
Plums, damson	5	0.9	30
Grapes	20	0.6	30
Watermelon	1 c	0.4	40
Juices			
Grape	1/2 c (4 oz)	0.6	80
Grapefruit	1/2 c (4 oz)	0.5	40
Orange	1/2 c (4 oz)	0.5	40
Apple	1/2 c (4 oz)	0.4	60
Vegetables			
Peas	1/2 c	3.6	60
Corn, canned	1/2 c	2.9	90

Fiber Content of Selected Foods

FOOD	SERVING SIZE	FIBER (GRAMS)	CALORIES
Parsnips	1/2 c	2.7	50
Potato (w/skin)	1 med	2.5	110
Carrots	1/2 c	2.3	20
Brussels sprouts	1/2 c	2.3	30
Broccoli	1/2 c	2.2	20
Spinach	1/2 c	2.0	20
Zucchini	1/2 c	1.8	10
Sweet potato	1/2 med	1.7	80
Beans, string, green	1/2 c	1.6	15
Turnip	1/2 c	1.6	20

Source: Lanza, E., and Butrum, R. (1986). A critical review of food fiber and data. *Journal of the American Dietetic Association, 86,* 732-740.

FLAVOR WITHOUT FAT

CHAPTER NINE

A Low Fat Kitchen

LOW FAT EATING

Low fat eating will benefit everyone, so it is a good idea to feed your entire family in this way. Start with changes that usually meet with little resistance, like giving everyone a glass of water with his meal, preparing two vegetables and serving fresh fruits as desserts or snacks.

Introduce a new recipe every other day and let everyone try it. Keep the mood happy. Prepare and serve the food so that it looks attractive and let your family know how much you enjoy its taste. Remember, as your family loses their taste for high fat, high sugar foods, they will accept and enjoy these changes.

Holiday and special occasion traditions may involve high fat foods. Whenever possible, change the tradition by introducing low fat food traditions. If that doesn't seem reasonable, modify the recipe by reducing the amounts of fats and sugars or simply eat a smaller portion of the original recipe.

To increase the convenience of low fat cooking, prepare double recipes of soups, casseroles, and breads. Freeze one recipe.

When grocery shopping, read the labels and learn exactly how many grams of fat are in the foods you are eating. Buy canned fruits and tuna that are marked "juice-packed" or "water-packed." Look for the low sodium variety of high sodium canned goods such as green beans or tomato juice. Buy low fat, low sugar foods. Give these eating changes top priority and you will be rewarded with more energy and better physical and mental health.

Put your pantry on a diet—permanently. "Dejunking" your kitchen and restocking it with light, nutritious ingredients are the first steps toward adapting your recipes and cooking style.

When shopping, don't just look for products tagged diet or all natural; instead, read and compare labels to determine which has the most nutritional value. Some imitation products may contain saturated palm or coconut oils, and others may not be significantly lower in fat or calories.

SUBSTITUTIONS

Bouillon granules: Chicken or beef granules can be added to water as a substitute for broth and are lower in fat and sodium than most canned broths.

Canned goods: Look for fruits packed in their own juice. No salt added canned vegetables are available. Use waterpacked seafood and rinse before using to reduce the sodium.

Cheese: A rich source of protein and calcium, cheese can be high in sodium and fat. Look for cheeses made with skim milk or, better yet, buy non-fat cheeses. Use Neufchatel instead of cream cheese to save 30 calories per ounce. Low fat cottage cheese can be substituted for ricotta in most recipes and is an excellent substitution for sour cream when whipped in the blender with a little skim milk or plain yogurt.

Cocoa powder: Use plain or Dutch processed cocoa powder instead of chocolate. Substitute one-fourth cup of cocoa and two teaspoons of vegetable oil for one square of baking chocolate.

Corn product: Stone ground white or yellow cornmeal has more nutrients than finer grinds.

Cornstarch: It can be used instead of cream, butter, or flour to thicken a sauce. Use half as much cornstarch as you would flour.

Egg substitute: All of the cholesterol is in the egg yolk, so when possible substitute two egg whites for each whole egg in a recipe. Cholesterol free egg substitutes are also available; use one-fourth cup egg substitute for a whole egg.

Herbs and spices: To enhance a recipe's flavor, use four parts fresh to one part dry herbs.

Legumes: Beans and peas are an inexpensive source of vegetable protein and fiber, and they contain very little fat.

Margarine: Made with unsaturated fat. Try cutting back on the amount of margarine in stir-fry and casserole recipes by a third or a half.

Milk: Use non-fat dry milk in coffee and tea. Equal amounts of skim or low fat milk can be substituted for whole milk and evaporated skim milk (184 calories per cup) will often work in place of whipping cream (838 calories per cup). Use skim or 1% milk. Two percent and whole milk have greater than 30% fat.

Oil: Always use vegetable oil, preferably sunflower, safflower, or corn oil.

Pasta and noodles: Stick to plain flour types where possible; egg noodles contain egg yolks.

Rice: Most white rice has been polished for longer shelf-life and then enriched with vitamins and minerals. Because these nutrients are applied to the outside of the rice, they can easily be lost by rinsing or by using too much water in the cooking process. Use brown rice.

Sugar: One teaspoon of firmly packed brown sugar has 17 calories; the same amount of granulated sugar has 16; and powdered sugar has 10. Try using one-third less sugar and adding more cinnamon, nutmeg, almond, or vanilla extract.

Tofu: An excellent source of vegetable protein, calcium, and iron that may help lower cholesterol. Tofu (soybean curd) can be added to stir-fry dishes, tossed in salads, and mixed into spreads and dips. Tofu is similar in nutritional value to cottage cheese, but has less sodium and more iron. Also, tofu is tasteless; it takes on the flavor of whatever you cook it with.

Vegetable cooking spray: Sauté with low fat spray instead of butter or oil.

Yogurt: Use plain low fat yogurt as a calcium-rich base for dips, dressings, and even desserts.

COOKING FOR NUTRITION

The shorter the cooking time for fruits and vegetables, the fewer nutrients are lost. Stir-frying and steaming are quick methods that keep the vitamin and mineral content high.

Grill or broil meats on a rack so that fat drains away, and be sure to trim all visible fat before cooking. Freeze steaks for an hour before slicing thinly across the grain for stir-frying. As you skin chicken parts, also remove the whitish fat pad beneath the skin.

Defat soups, stews, and gravies by making them ahead of time and chilling them until the fat congeals. You'll save 100 calories for each tablespoon of fat you lift off.

Before cooking, rinse sodium and oil from canned vegetables and tuna. Replace salt with herbs and spices. Chives, parsley, and tarragon are good with most vegetables; onion, garlic, thyme, sage, rosemary, and oregano flavor meats, fish, and poultry. Cook with wine; the flavor remains during cooking while the alcohol evaporates and calories are reduced.

SNEAKY SNACKS

America loves to snack. This is often the primary reason why most people are overweight. If you are watching your weight, it is important to eat three meals a day so snacking is kept to a minimum.

In general, snacks are high in fat. Chips, crackers,

dips, pizza, and ice cream lead the way. In the past, low fat snacking usually meant low fat, tasteless munchies.

Today, low fat snacking is a breeze. Thanks to people like George Mateljan at Health Valley, we can keep our snacking habits and enjoy low sodium, high fiber, delicious treats. Some of the fine foods by Health Valley include fat-free crackers, cookies, muffins, and much more. Your supermarket may carry some fat-free products, but your local natural food stores usually offer the greatest selection.

Other tips:

1. Keep sliced fruit, as well as whole fresh fruit, available.

2. Keep prepared, raw vegetables available.

3. Keep a variety of low fat breads, rolls, and muffins available.

4. Encourage snacking on low sugar cereals, either dry or with skim milk.

5. Encourage snacking on plain, low fat yogurt with fruit, cereal, or bread.

6. Make popsicles out of fruit juice.

CHAPTER TEN

Eating Out

As a rule, Americans eat two out of three meals away from home. The restaurant industry is slowly recognizing the demand for healthier, low fat alternatives. When eating out, remember not to eat with abandonment; instead take a few minutes and make some wise choices.

The following are suggestions on how to meet this challenge:

1. For breakfast, ask for hot cereal or whole wheat toast without butter, a grapefruit, orange, or fresh juice.

2. For lunch, order a non-cream soup or a salad with lots of chunky vegetables topped with lemon juice. Of course, you could always order some kind of baked fish or chicken with baked potato and vegetable. Replace french fries with sliced tomatoes.

3. Choosing a low fat dinner is not too difficult. Baked halibut, teriyaki chicken, soup, or salad are all good dinner choices. Vegetable plates or Chinese foods are usually low in fat, too. Avoid high fat desserts. Select fruit or sherbet.

4. Be careful with salad dressings. Always have your dressing on the side. Use a little oil and a lot of vinegar. Avoid creamy dressings. Try an

alternative such as lemon, dill, oregano, and sage to add zest to your salads without fat.

5. At a restaurant, have an appetizer such as clear soup, shrimp cocktail, or fresh fruit to decrease your appetite. Control the bread you eat. Enjoy only one piece of bread with your meal, not a basket before your meal.

6. Use alcohol in moderation. It has little or no nutritional value, but plenty of calories. If you must have a social drink, the best is white wine, which is lowest in calories. A better idea is to combine white wine with club soda with a twist of lemon or lime. This drink is called a Spritzer and is lower in calories than a plain glass of white wine. After white wine, the drink lowest in calories is rosé, followed by red wine, light beer, wine coolers, regular beer, whiskey, and liqueurs. Avoid creme drinks such as Brandy Alexanders, Pink Squirrels, etc. These are extremely high in fat and calories.

7. Choose the restaurant so you can better anticipate the available menu. Call ahead if you don't know about the menu. Avoid all-you-can-eat restaurants.

8. Be assertive. Ask how food is prepared or served and, if necessary, request appropriate modifications.

   • Ask for dressings or sauces to be served on the side.
   • Ask that unwanted food be removed or not served (potato chips, rolls, pickles, french fries).

- Ask that food be prepared with no added fat.

9. If unwanted food is served, ask that it be removed or make it inedible by liberally sprinkling it with salt, pepper, or sugar.

10. If portion size is too large, share your order with another person or take home a doggie bag. Ordering items a la carte is also helpful. Soup and salad, or two appetizers, can be a meal in itself.

11. Exercise a little more on the days you plan to eat out to accommodate any extra calories.

12. Focus on enjoying the company with whom you're dining instead of just the food. Substitute non-food-related activities for socializing. Not every celebration has to include food.

13. Eat slowly! Put your fork down between bites. Talk to the others at the table.

14. Enlist support when you go out to eat. Ask others not to encourage you to eat foods for which you have not planned and to reinforce the choices you have made.

FLAVOR WITHOUT FAT

CHAPTER ELEVEN

A Word on Vitamins

VITAMINS

Vitamins are often misunderstood substances. Proponents claim vitamins and minerals work wonders in providing zest and energy. Opponents claim they are a waste of money and not needed if people eat a good diet. Where is the truth?

Consider this:

MYTH: Food provides all the vitamins a person needs.

FACT: Very, very few people eat three balanced meals on a daily basis. Furthermore, with the way produce is grown and rushed to markets, coupled with how food is processed, the vitamin content is sadly lacking. And don't be fooled by words like "Enriched." Enriched bread, for example, means they have taken 17 nutrients out and put back 14. Does that sound like they did you a favor?

MYTH: If you take vitamins, you just pass them out in your urine.

FACT: If you drink a glass of water, it passes out in your urine also. But everyone knows the profound importance of drinking water and the serious consequences, including death, caused by dehydration. True, drinking water ultimately results in its passing out in the urine, but it has tremendous therapeutic benefits while passing through the body. So do vitamins.

MYTH: Vitamins have side effects.

FACT: All drugs, prescriptions, as well as over-the-counter, have many side effects. Even small dosages often considered safe can cause problems. The side effects of vitamins are seen in very few people and generally only when taken in tremendous excess. Furthermore, only a very few vitamins (the fat soluble ones—A, D, E, and K) have been shown to cause problems and again only when taken in extremely high dosages. Unlike drugs, the majority of vitamins are very, very safe.

MYTH: People have died from taking vitamins.

FACT: From 1981 to 1990, *The Journal of Emergency Room Medicine* reported zero deaths from vitamins and minerals.

MYTH: My doctor said there was no need to take vitamins.

FACT: The training to become an M.D. (Medical Doctor) is focused on treating, not preventing, disease. Vitamin therapy is best researched and understood by physicians specializing in Preventive Medicine.

Vitamins are not medicines. And though they are involved in healing, they are not drugs. Vitamins are not a substitute for food. In fact, you must have food for your body to use vitamins.

How do vitamins work? Think of your body as a complex and sophisticated chemical plant. Vitamins are essential for millions of chemical reactions that go on inside your body. These chemical reactions regulate metabolism and maintain all body functions including the heart, liver, and kidneys. Vitamins are found in very small quantities in the food. Therefore, it is wise to take a vitamin supplement.

SUPPLEMENTS

In selecting a vitamin/mineral supplement, read the label carefully. Make sure you're getting 100 % of RDA of each vitamin and most of the minerals. Read the fine print. Some manufacturers suggest three pills a day to obtain the daily RDA. This seems inconvenient, but think about it. It is not wise to eat only once a day, so taking a vitamin just one time a day may not always be the best choice. The selection of vitamins available is overwhelming and confusing. Take a supplement that is suited for your individual needs. The best place to make your choice is in a natural food store where the staff is educated and trained to help you. Many common one-a-day-vitamins are not complete supplements and contain sugar and other additives.

INDIGESTION

Some people suffer from vitamin burp. After taking vitamins, they belch and can taste the vitamins. This is sometimes due to the binders and fillers present. First, be sure your vitamin has none of these additives. If the problem persists, take your vitamins before going to bed.

ALLERGIES

A few people seem to experience an allergic reaction when they take vitamins. This is not because they are allergic to vitamins, although most people think that's the case. Rather, they are allergic to the food coloring, fillers or binders in the tablet, or even the coating on the outside of the tablet, which is sometimes made of coal tar.

If you think you suffered an allergic reaction, try another brand. Ask your natural foods expert to help you find one without all the "junk"—a supplement that is free of artificial coloring, sugar, yeast, and other additives.

CALCIUM

Calcium is needed for the repair of bones and joints, a process your body undergoes every day. If you drink a lot of milk and eat a lot of dairy products such as cheese, chances are you're getting all the calcium you need. But why take chances? And, besides, cheese is high in fat. Also, many people eat irregularly and don't get enough calcium. For them, a daily calcium supplement is a good way to ensure they're getting enough of this important mineral. It's particularly important to take a calcium supplement while losing weight.

As with a vitamin supplement, make sure you read labels carefully. The fine print often tells a different story than the larger type on the label. For example, while the calcium label might say the tablet contains 500 milligrams of calcium, the fine print reads the 500 milligrams of calcium in each table is equivalent to 200 milligrams of elemental or available calcium.

It is this elemental or available calcium that your body needs—a total of 1,000 to 1,200 milligrams a day. If the label says nothing about elemental or available calcium, then rest assured that all of the calcium in the tablet is elemental or available. Only those calcium supplements that are not made totally with elemental or available calcium will list an amount in the fine print.

Women over 30 should take 1,000 to 1,200 milligrams a day. In addition, the latest research shows that your body only absorbs 300 milligrams of calcium at a time. Therefore, taking a supplement with 300 milligrams several times a day is preferred over a 500 or 600 milligrams supplement twice a day.

Finally, some calcium brands are more easily absorbed than others. Here's a simple test to find out if the calcium you bought will be easily absorbed into your body. Drop one tablet of calcium supplement into a shot glass full of vinegar. That's right—vinegar. The tablet should be completely dissolved in 30 minutes with no residue left at all. Your stomach is an acid medium and calcium must have acid present to be absorbed. If the tablet does not dissolve, it's not a good supplement.

Controversy exists over the use of chewable antacids

as a calcium source. As previously mentioned, calcium needs to be in an acid environment to be absorbed. It doesn't make sense to take an antacid and calcium together. A final note, people with a history of kidney stones generally should not take calcium supplements.

CHAPTER TWELVE

Low Fat Cooking

EATING RIGHT STARTS WITH COOKING RIGHT

Eating healthier starts in the kitchen. Give the frying pan a heave. Put it way in the back of the cupboard. You don't need it. Frying is one of the worst ways to cook foods (with some exceptions, such as stir-fry meals or browning meat for stews, etc.).

Instead of fried chicken, try baked chicken. Instead of fried hamburgers, try broiled hamburgers. Instead of fried hot dogs, try boiled hot dogs.

You should hardly ever use your frying pan. The problem with frying is that you often use oil or, worse yet, butter or lard. And much of the fat doesn't drip away or burn off with frying. The food just sits in the grease and fat. *Grease and fat are two deadly enemies!*

If you must use your frying pan, use a cooking spray instead of margarine or oil. Avoid butter and lard; *excess saturated fats are extremely harmful to your health.*

STEAMING

Vegetables steam nicely because you can control their cooking time so they will be crunchy. Try it this way, and you will really get the full flavor of the vegetable. Do not steam them too much. The more you cook a vegetable, the higher the calories. A lot of heat breaks down the cellulose fiber in the vegetable, and this allows your body to more easily absorb the vegetable's calories.

There is another plus to steaming: It leaves you with great, tasty juices you can use in many ways. Save the water left in the pan after steaming vegetables. Use that water as a starter for soup stock, to boil pasta or rice, to mix with gravies, and in many other ways. Many nutrients are left in the water, too, so don't throw those nutrients down the drain. Save them and add flavor to your cooking at the same time. Keep jars of this water in the refrigerator and use it instead of tap water in all cooking.

Remember not to overcook your vegetables—broccoli, for example, should be a little crunchy. The same is true of carrots.

MICROWAVE COOKING

This is another excellent way to prepare most food. But the biggest problem is that people tend to overcook in a microwave. Understand that food continues cooking after you take it out of the microwave, and you have to allow for this when figuring cooking time.

There are several good microwave cookbooks on the market. Use them to help you avoid soggy baked potatoes, hard bread, and overcooked meat.

BOILING

New England boiled dinner is just one of many, many examples of the fine meals you can prepare by boiling. You have to work at ruining a meal by boiling—that's how easy it is. And, remember, save your water. It's a great starter for stock.

CROCK POT COOKING

It's mouth-watering just thinking about meals, cooking slowly all day in their own juices. Once you get used to cooking foods in natural juices, you will use fewer spices, especially salt.

Several crock pot cookbooks have excellent recipes for meals you can prepare the night before and then put in the crock pot before leaving for work in the morning. When you come home, dinner's ready!

BAKING

You cannot go wrong baking your food. Use baking as the main alternative to frying. You can bake almost anything that calls for frying. Some people complain that baked foods dry out, particularly roasts and chicken.

Remember those vegetable juices you have saved in the refrigerator? Put them in with your roast, and cover the roast in a baking pan. The moist heat bakes the roast to a tender and tasty treat.

Wrap your meat in aluminum foil with water or broth and watch how tender it turns out.

Soups add pizzazz to many dishes in the oven; cream of mushroom and chicken soups are great combinations if you are tired of dried-out baked chicken that tastes like straw. Remember to mix cream soups with water, not milk.

Cooking with juices, sauces, and soups will allow you to buy lean cuts of meat. Avoid meats heavily marbled with fat; such foods only add fat calories and cholesterol to your diet.

In many dishes such as peas or beans, people often add animal fat. Consider dropping a few pods of okra in the beginning to give the dish that "fat feel." These can easily be removed prior to serving.

Finally, limit the prepared foods you and your family eat. This is hard in our modern society, when families are on the go. But many of these prepared foods have too much salt, sugar, and calories. Meals made from scratch have more nutrition, and, most importantly, taste better. When shopping, stay on the outer aisles of the market for most of what you'll need—produce, meats, poultry, fish, breads, dairy products, and other essentials. The prepared, canned, and frozen foods are on all the inside aisles.

Finally, nutritious meals don't have to be bland. Quite

the contrary. And remember, cooking is a learning experience. The more you do it, the better your meals taste. Don't give up if your first low fat meal isn't fabulous. Practice makes perfect.

Bon Appetit!

FLAVOR WITHOUT FAT

Chapter 13

Salads

For Healthy Living

MACARONI SALAD

1 cup	whole wheat macaroni, uncooked
2 Tbsp	low fat cottage cheese, blended
2 Tbsp	fat-free mayonnaise
1 Tbsp	vinegar
1 tsp	prepared mustard
3/4 cup	celery, chopped
6 reg	green onions, sliced
2 Tbsp	sweet pickle relish
1 Tbsp	pimento, chopped

1. Boil and drain macaroni.
2. Mix blended cottage cheese, fat-free mayonnaise, vinegar, and mustard in a large bowl.
3. Add remaining ingredients and toss together. Chill before serving.

Serves 8

Calories per serving:	132
Protein:	6 gm
Carbohydrate:	27 gm
Fat:	2 gm=14%

TUNA AND BEAN SALAD

1	20-oz can kidney beans
1/4 cup	onion, finely chopped
1/2 tsp	garlic, minced
1/2 tsp	dried oregano
2 Tbsp	parsley flakes
1 Tbsp	red wine vinegar
1/4 cup	no oil Italian dressing
1 tsp	lemon juice
Dash	salt and pepper
2	7-oz cans tuna, water-packed

1. In a bowl, combine all of the above ingredients except the tuna. Toss lightly.
2. Add the tuna. Toss lightly. Serve with tomato slices.

Serves 6

Calories per serving:	205
Protein:	30 gm
Carbohydrate:	17 gm
Fat:	2 gm=9%

COLESLAW GELATIN

2 envelopes	gelatin, unflavored
1/2 cup	cold water
1 cup	water
1 cup	apple juice
2 Tbsp	lemon juice
3 Tbsp	onion, chopped
1 cup	cabbage, shredded
1 cup	celery, diced
3 Tbsp	pimento, chopped
3 Tbsp	green pepper, chopped

1. Soften unflavored gelatin in 1/2 cup cold water.
2. Add 1 cup water. Heat to boiling. Cool slightly and add apple juice and lemon juice.
3. Continue cooling until mixture starts to thicken.
4. Fold in onion, cabbage, celery, pimento, and green pepper.
5. Pour into a 1-quart mold and chill until set. Serve.

Serves 8

Calories per serving:	33
Protein:	2 gm
Carbohydrate:	6 gm
Fat:	Trace

CUCUMBER AND ONION MARINADE

1 med	cucumber, peeled and sliced
1 med	onion, thinly sliced
1/4 cup	vinegar
1/4 cup	water
Dash	paprika
Dash	black pepper

1. Combine all ingredients.
2. Chill before serving. Stir occasionally.

Serves 4

Calories per serving:	16
Protein:	1 gm
Carbohydrate:	4 gm
Fat:	Trace

SEVEN LAYER SALAD

1	head of lettuce, shredded
1	green pepper, diced
5	stalks celery, chopped
1/2	onion, chopped
10 oz	frozen peas
1 cup	low fat yogurt, or
1 cup	low fat cottage cheese, blended, or
1 cup	any creamy low fat salad dressing
2 Tbsp	sugar
2 Tbsp	grated Parmesan cheese
2 Tbsp	imitation bacon bits
2	tomatoes, wedged

1. Put shredded lettuce into a bowl. Layer diced green pepper, chopped celery, chopped onion, and peas on top of lettuce.
2. Spread yogurt or blended cottage cheese completely over the top of the salad.
3. Sprinkle with sugar, Parmesan cheese, and bacon bits. Garnish with tomato wedges.
4. Cover lightly and chill, preferably overnight. Toss thoroughly before serving.

Serves 6

Calories per serving:	73
Protein:	4 gm
Carbohydrate:	13 gm
Fat:	1 gm=12%

WALDORF SALAD

2 Tbsp	lemon juice
2 cups	apples, unpeeled, diced
2 cups	celery, diced
1 cup	seedless grapes, halved
1/2 cup	pineapple tidbits, juice packed, liquid drained and reserved
1/2 cup	low fat cottage cheese
2 Tbsp	non-fat dry milk
1 Tbsp	walnuts, chopped (optional)
	lettuce leaves

1. Sprinkle lemon juice on diced apples to keep them white.
2. Toss apples, celery, grapes, and pineapple together gently.
3. Place cottage cheese, non-fat dry milk and 1 Tbsp drained liquid from pineapple tidbits into blender. Blend until creamy smooth.
4. Pour over apple mixture and toss until thoroughly mixed.
5. Chill. Serve on lettuce leaves. Sprinkle 1/2 tsp walnuts over each serving, if desired.
6. For a crispy combination, mix only pineapple, apples, celery, and walnuts together and serve.

Serves 4

Calories per serving:	76
Protein:	5 gm
Carbohydrate:	11 gm
Fat:	1/2 gm=17%

HAWAIIAN CHICKEN SALAD

2 cups	chicken or turkey, cooked and diced
2	apples, peeled and diced
1 cup	pineapple chunks, drained
3 Tbsp	low fat cottage cheese, blended
6	lettuce leaves
Garnish	almonds, chopped

1. Toss together all ingredients, except almonds and lettuce leaves.
2. Spoon individual portions onto lettuce leaves.
3. Garnish each with 1 chopped almond before serving.

Serves 6

Calories per serving:	138
Protein:	16 gm
Carbohydrate:	15 gm
Fat:	2 1/2 gm=17%

CHUNK CHICKEN SALAD

2 cups	chicken or turkey, cooked and diced
1/2	cucumber, peeled and diced
1/2 cup	celery, diced
1/2 cup	water chestnuts, drained and sliced
1/4 cup	green pepper, diced
1/4 cup	pimento, chopped
6	green onions, sliced
1/4 cup	low fat cottage cheese, blended
6	lettuce leaves
Sprinkle	paprika

1. Toss chicken, cucumber, celery, water chestnuts, green pepper, pimento, and green onions with blended cottage cheese.
2. Serve on lettuce leaves with a sprinkle of paprika.

Serves 6

Calories per serving:	107
Protein:	15 gm
Carbohydrate:	6 gm
Fat:	2 gm=18%

SHRIMP SALAD

1 lb	shrimp, cleaned
1/2	onion, peeled and sliced
1	5 oz can water chestnuts, sliced
4 Tbsp	low calorie Italian dressing
1 tsp	dill, dried, or
2 Tbsp	fresh dill, chopped
1 head	romaine lettuce
3	tomatoes
4 oz	mushrooms, sliced
Garnish	parsley

1. Drain and chill shrimp.
2. Toss shrimp, onion, water chestnuts, and dressing. Sprinkle with dill.
3. Serve on romaine lettuce. Surround with sliced tomatoes and mushrooms. Garnish with parsley.

Serves 10

Calories per serving:	85
Protein:	12 gm
Carbohydrate:	7 gm
Fat:	less than 1 gm=5%

SWEET AND SOUR SALAD

1 med	red cabbage (1 1/2 lbs), cored and sliced thin
1 large	tart apple, peeled, cored, and cut into 1/2-inch cubes
1 small	sweet green pepper, cored, seeded, and sliced lengthwise into strips about 1/4-inch wide
1 small	yellow onion, chopped fine
1/2 cup	red wine vinegar
1 Tbsp	honey
1/2 tsp	caraway seeds
1/8 tsp	black pepper
1/8 tsp	ground cloves

1. In a large heatproof bowl, combine the cabbage, apple, green pepper, and onion and toss well to mix; set aside.
2. In a small saucepan over moderate heat, cook and stir the vinegar, honey, caraway seeds, black pepper, and cloves until the mixture just begins to boil—about one minute.
3. Pour the hot mixture over the salad and toss well. Let stand at room temperature for 30 minutes before serving.

Serves 7

Calories per serving:	77
Protein:	2 gm
Carbohydrate:	21 gm
Fat:	less than 1 gm=11%

ORIENTAL SHRIMP SALAD

4 cups	chicken stock
1	8 oz pkg buckwheat noodles
3 cups	fresh spinach leaves
3 cups	bibb lettuce
1/2 lb	medium shrimp, cooked and shelled
1/2 lb	snow peas, steamed 2 or 3 minutes or until crisp-tender
1/2 lb	asparagus
3	carrots, sliced diagonally into 4 or 5 pieces and steamed 3-4 minutes
1/2	English cucumber, peeled and thinly sliced
1 small	bunch radishes, trimmed and thinly sliced
1/2 cup	canned water chestnuts, drained balsamic vinaigrette

1. In a medium saucepan, bring chicken stock to a boil.
2. Add noodles and boil 5-7 minutes or until noodles are tender. Drain.
3. Arrange spinach and lettuce leaves over chilled salad plates. Mound noodles to one side of each plate. Arrange shrimp next to noodles.
4. Surround with snow peas, asparagus, carrots, and cucumber. Garnish with radishes and water chestnuts.
5. Serve hot or cold with balsamic vinaigrette.

Serves 5

Calories per serving:	319
Protein:	26 gm
Carbohydrate:	47 gm
Fat:	6 gm=17%

SHRIMP AND SPINACH SALAD

1/2 cup	cooked shrimp, shelled
1	English cucumber, very thinly sliced
1/4 cup	rice vinegar
1 tsp	reduced-sodium soy sauce
1 Tbsp	granulated sugar
1/2 tsp	salt
10	fresh spinach leaves, stems removed, steamed and chilled

1. In a salad bowl, combine the shrimp and cucumber.
2. In a jar with cover, combine vinegar, soy sauce, sugar, and salt, and pour over shrimp and cucumber. Chill 1 hour.
3. Just before serving, mix in spinach. Spoon into small bowls or custard cups. Serve with chopsticks.

Serves 6

Calories per serving:	38
Protein:	5 gm
Carbohydrate:	4 gm
Fat:	Trace

CHICKEN, SHRIMP, AND PASTA SALAD

1/4 head	cauliflower, florets only
2	carrots, peeled and thinly sliced diagonally
1/2 lb	snow peas
1	leek, thinly sliced
1 head	bibb lettuce
1 lb	cavatelli or other shell-shaped pasta, cooked *al dente*
1	chicken breast, skinned, boned, poached, and cut into strips 1/2-inch wide
8 med	prawns, cooked and shelled.
1	7 oz can water-packed artichoke hearts, drained
	balsamic vinaigrette

1. Separately blanch cauliflower, carrots, snow peas, and leek 1-2 minutes or just until crisp-tender.
2. Arrange lettuce over dinner plates. Mound pasta, chicken, prawns, and vegetables over lettuce. Serve with balsamic vinaigrette.

Serves 8

Calories per serving:	124
Protein:	7 gm
Carbohydrate:	22 gm
Fat:	Trace

PASTA AND BEAN SALAD

2	15 oz cans kidney beans, drained and rinsed
1	15 oz can black beans, drained and rinsed
2 large	tomatoes, coarsely chopped
1	red onion, coarsely chopped
2 cups	cavatelli or other shell-shaped pasta, cooked *al dente*
2 Tbsp	white wine vinegar
3/4 tsp	salt
1/4 tsp	black pepper
3	cloves garlic, minced
1/2 cup	fresh basil (optional)

1. Mix all ingredients, toss well, and sprinkle with the vinegar.

Serves 8

Calories per serving:	84
Protein:	4 gm
Carbohydrate:	13 gm
Fat:	2 gm=22%

VEGETABLE ANTIPASTO

1 clove	garlic, minced
1/4 cup	fresh lemon juice
1 Tbsp	olive oil
1/2 tsp	salt
1/4 tsp	black pepper
4 small	carrots, diagonally sliced
1 small	zucchini, peeled and sliced on the diagonal into matchstick strips
1/4 lb	broccoli florets
6	tiny red potatoes, quartered
1/4 lb	fresh green beans
1/2	red onion, cut into rings
6	plum tomatoes, quartered

1. In a covered jar, combine garlic, lemon juice, olive oil, salt, and pepper. Set aside.
2. In a steamer over boiling water, steam vegetables, one type at a time, just until crisp-tender: carrots, zucchini, and broccoli about 2 minutes each; potatoes and green beans about 6-10 minutes each. As each vegetable is cooked, remove to a 13x9x2-inch glass casserole dish.
3. Tuck onion rings and tomatoes among vegetables as garnish.
4. Chill at least 3 hours. Just before serving, toss with dressing.

Serves 8

Calories per serving:	112
Protein:	3 gm
Carbohydrate:	22 gm
Fat:	2 gm=16%

BLACK BEANS WITH VEGETABLES AND SHRIMP

1 1/2 cups	salsa
1 cup	black bean dip
2/3 lb	medium prawns, cooked, shelled, and deveined
1	English cucumber, thinly sliced
8 stalks	celery, sliced diagonally into thirds
8	carrots, sliced diagonally into thirds
	fresh parsley for garnish
1	lime, cut into wedges
1	1-inch square pieces of tomato for garnish

1. Into the center of a medium dish, spread 1/2 cup of the salsa.
2. Mound bean dip over salsa.
3. Arrange prawns, cucumber, celery, and carrots around dip. Tuck in parsley and lime wedges for garnish.
4. Top bean dip with small pieces of tomato and touch of parsley.
5. Pour remaining cup of salsa into bowl and pass with vegetables.

Serves 6

Calories per serving:	183
Protein:	17 gm
Carbohydrate:	28 gm
Fat:	2 gm=10%

81

GEORGETOWN RICE SALAD

4 1/2 cups	chicken broth
3 cups	long grain brown rice, uncooked
1/4 cup	olive oil
2 Tbsp	rice vinegar
1 tsp	dry mustard
3/4 tsp	salt or to taste
1/2 tsp	black pepper
1	yellow or red pepper, diced
1	green pepper, diced
3 large	ripe tomatoes, diced

1. In a medium saucepan, bring chicken stock to a boil.
2. Add rice, cover, reduce heat, and simmer 20-30 minutes or until rice is tender and moisture is absorbed. Cool. Spoon into a low salad bowl.
3. In a jar with cover, combine olive oil, vinegar, mustard, salt, and pepper. Pour over rice and toss.
4. Sprinkle diced peppers and tomatoes over rice. Toss again. Chill.

Serves 10

Calories per serving:	139
Protein:	3 gm
Carbohydrate:	24 gm
Fat:	3 gm=19%

WINTER VEGETABLE SALAD

3 cups	romaine lettuce, torn into bite-size pieces
1 1/2 cups	bibb lettuce, torn into bite-size pieces
1 1/2 cups	iceberg lettuce, torn into bite-size pieces
6	mushrooms, sliced
2 med	tomatoes, cut into wedges
1/2	red onion, thinly sliced into rings
	non-fat creamy garlic dressing

1. Layer lettuce onto chilled salad plates.
2. Arrange mushrooms, tomatoes, and onion rings over top. Drizzle with dressing.

Serves 4

Calories per serving:	30
Protein:	2 gm
Carbohydrate:	6 gm
Fat:	Trace

SPINACH AND ONION SALAD

3 cloves	garlic
6 Tbsp	fresh lemon juice
1/4 cup	olive oil
3/4 tsp	salt or to taste
1 bunch	fresh spinach leaves, torn into bite-size pieces
1/2	white onion, thinly sliced into rings
	non-fat salad dressing

1. In a blender or food processor, combine garlic, lemon juice, olive oil, and salt.
2. In a salad bowl, toss spinach and onion with desired amount of non-fat salad dressing.

Serves 6

Calories per serving:	20
Protein:	2 gm
Carbohydrate:	3 gm
Fat:	Trace

SUMMER FRUIT SALAD

3	leaves, red or green leaf lettuce
1/2 cup	non-fat vanilla yogurt
3 large	ripe strawberries, thinly sliced
3 slices	fresh peaches
1 slice	fresh pineapple, cut into chunks
1 small	wedge cantaloupe, cubed
1 small	wedge honeydew melon, cubed
1 small	wedge watermelon, cubed

1. Layer the lettuce on a chilled dinner plate.
2. Spoon yogurt into individual custard cup or soufflé bowl; place on center or side of plate.
3. Surround with fresh fruit.

Serves 2

Calories per serving:	74
Protein:	4 gm
Carbohydrate:	14 gm
Fat:	Trace

FLAVOR WITHOUT FAT

Chapter 14

Soups

For Healthy Living

TACO BEAN SOUP

6 cups	pinto beans, cooked
1 med	onion, chopped
2 cloves	garlic, chopped
1/4 tsp	black pepper
1/2 tsp	cumin seeds
1	4 oz can taco sauce
1	4 oz can diced green chilies
2 cups	tomatoes, stewed

1. Combine all ingredients.
2. Adjust with water so soup has desired consistency.
3. Bring to a boil. Reduce heat and simmer 1 hour. Serve hot.

Serves 12

Calories per serving:	149
Protein:	8 gm
Carbohydrate:	27 gm
Fat:	less than 1 gm=4%

COUNTRY BEAN SOUP

2 cups	navy beans, dried
4 oz	lean ham, baked and cubed
1/2 cup	mashed potatoes
3 cups	celery, chopped
4 med	onions, chopped
3 Tbsp	fresh parsley, chopped
1 clove	garlic, minced
1/2 cup	skim milk
1/2 cup	carrots, diced
To taste	black pepper

1. Cover beans with water and soak overnight in soup pot. Drain.
2. Add ham and cover with water again. Cover and bring to a boil; reduce heat, and simmer 1 hour.
3. Add remaining ingredients; simmer 1 hour more or until beans are tender. Serve hot.

Serves 12

Calories per serving:	170
Protein:	5 gm
Carbohydrate:	12 gm
Fat:	1.9 gm=10%

CREAM OF CHICKEN SOUP

1 cup	chicken
1/2 cup	celery, chopped
1/2 cup	onion, chopped
1/2 cup	mushrooms, chopped
2 Tbsp	cornstarch
5 cups	chicken stock
1 cup	skim milk

1. Cook chicken until tender. Remove meat from bones and cut into bite-size pieces.
2. Sauté celery, onions, and mushrooms.
3. Whisk cornstarch into cool chicken stock. Add milk, chicken, and vegetables. Heat, stirring constantly, until thick and creamy. Serve.

Serves 6

Calories per serving:	91
Protein:	12 gm
Carbohydrate:	8 gm
Fat:	1 gm=10%

SUNSHINE SOUP

2 cups	squash, cooked and mashed
2	onions, chopped
1 cup	celery, chopped
1 clove	garlic, minced
1/2 tsp	rosemary
1 qt	chicken stock
1/4 tsp	black pepper
2 cups	skim milk
Garnish	nutmeg

1. Combine all ingredients except milk in a soup pot. Cook until onions and celery are tender.
2. Remove from heat, add milk, sprinkle with nutmeg, and serve immediately.

Serves 6

Calories per serving:	66
Protein:	5 gm
Carbohydrate:	13 gm
Fat:	Trace

CAULIFLOWER SOUP

1/3 cup	brown rice, raw
2 cups	cauliflower, cut into pieces
5 cups	chicken stock
1/2 cup	celery, chopped
4 Tbsp	cornstarch
1 cup	skim milk
Garnish	chives, parsley, or watercress

1. Cook rice.
2. Bring cauliflower, stock, and celery to boil. Reduce heat and simmer until cauliflower is crisp-tender, about 10 minutes.
3. Whisk cornstarch into milk until smooth. Add to soup, stirring constantly, and heat until thickened.
4. Add seasoning and rice. Garnish with chives, parsley or watercress and serve.

VARIATION:
Broccoli Soup—Prepare as directed with 2 cups of broccoli instead of cauliflower.

Serves 6

Calories per serving:	63
Protein:	4 gm
Carbohydrate:	11 gm
Fat:	less than 1 gm=7%

SIX BEAN MINESTRONE

1/2 cup	pinto beans, dried
1/2 cup	northern white beans, dried
1/2 cup	lima beans, dried
1 cup	red and pink beans, dried
10 cups	water
1/2 cup	garbanzo beans, canned
1	onion, chopped
1 clove	garlic, minced
2 cups	celery, chopped
1/4 cup	parsley, chopped
4 cups	tomatoes, stewed
2 cups	cabbage, shredded
5 cups	zucchini, thinly sliced

1. Soak all beans except garbanzos in 10 cups water overnight. Add more water as necessary. Change water before cooking beans. Cook beans 2 to 3 hours or until done. Add garbanzos and heat thoroughly.
2. Sauté onion, garlic, celery, and parsley.
3. Add tomatoes. Simmer, covered, for 45 minutes.
4. Add cabbage and zucchini. Add enough water to equal 7 1/2 quarts of soup. Cook until zucchini and cabbage are done. Serve hot.

Serves 16

Calories per serving:	78
Protein:	4 gm
Carbohydrate:	13 gm
Fat:	1 gm=11%

BLACK BEAN SOUP

4 cups	chicken broth
6 cloves	garlic
1 med	onion, chopped
1 cup	celery, chopped
1 tsp	ground coriander
1/4 tsp	ground red pepper
1/4 tsp	salt
3	15 oz cans black beans, drained

1. In a medium pot, simmer chicken broth, garlic, onion, celery, and seasonings 1 hour.
2. In a blender or food processor, puree 1 can of the black beans; add to stock pot.
3. Stir in remaining 2 cans of beans and heat through.

Serves 10

Calories per serving:	125
Protein:	9 gm
Carbohydrate:	20 gm
Fat:	1 gm=7%

SOUP LIBERATORE

20 oz	Italian plum tomatoes, diced
1 cup	bloody mary mix
1 cup	beef stock
1 Tbsp	lemon juice, freshly squeezed
5 cloves	garlic
1/2 cup	white onion, chopped
1/2 tsp	ground cumin
1/2 tsp	Tabasco sauce
1/2 tsp	crushed basil
3 cups	kidney beans
1 cup	green pepper, chopped
2 cups	elbow macaroni, cooked

1. In a small pot, combine tomatoes, bloody mary mix, beef stock, lemon juice, garlic, onion, cumin, hot sauce, and basil. Heat to just boiling. Then reduce heat and simmer 25 minutes.
2. Stir in beans and green pepper, and simmer 10 minutes.
3. Add macaroni and heat through.

Serves 12

Calories per serving:	98
Protein:	5 gm
Carbohydrate:	18 gm
Fat:	1 gm=9%

LENTIL SOUP

8 cups	chicken broth
1	6 oz can tomato paste
2 med	carrots, diced
1 large	potato, diced
1 large	onion, chopped
3 cloves	garlic, minced
1/4 tsp	powdered thyme
1 cup	lentils
3/4 tsp	salt or to taste

1. In a medium pot, bring chicken broth, tomato paste, carrots, potato, onion, garlic, and thyme to just boiling.
2. Add lentils and reduce heat, cover and simmer 1 1/2-2 hours or until lentils are cooked. Season with salt.

Serves 14

Calories per serving:	55
Protein:	3 gm
Carbohydrate:	10 gm
Fat:	Trace

TWO MUSHROOM SOUP

3 cups	chicken broth
1	6 oz can straw mushrooms, drained
1	8 oz can button mushrooms, drained

1. In a saucepan, heat chicken broth to just boiling. Stir in mushrooms. Simmer 5 minutes. Ladle into bowl.

Serves 4

Calories per serving:	48
Protein:	5 gm
Carbohydrate:	4 gm
Fat:	1 gm=19%

SOUP TORTELLINI

8 cups	chicken broth
1 cup	peas, cooked 1-2 minutes
1 cup	carrots, cut into julienne strips 1-inch long and cooked 2-3 minutes or just until crisp-tender
1	8 oz-can mushroom stems and pieces, drained
2/3 lb	tortellini, cooked *al dente*
1/2 cup	Parmesan cheese, freshly grated

1. In a medium pot, bring chicken broth to just boiling.
2. Add peas, carrots, mushrooms, and pasta. Ladle into bowls. Sprinkle with Parmesan.

Serves 15

Calories per serving:	196
Protein:	17 gm
Carbohydrate:	20 gm
Fat:	5 gm=22%

SEAFOOD GAZPACHO

1	28-oz can Italian plum tomatoes, diced
1 cup	bloody mary mix
1/2 cup	cucumber, peeled and chopped
1/3 cup	green pepper, chopped
1/2 cup	white onion, chopped
1 cup	beef broth
1 Tbsp	lemon juice, freshly squeezed
2 tsp	olive oil
1 Tbsp	garlic (5 whole cloves), minced
1/2 tsp	ground cumin
1/2 tsp	hot sauce
1/2 tsp	salt
1/2 tsp	crushed basil
1/2 lb	shrimp meat, cooked

1. In a large glass bowl, combine all the ingredients except shrimp.
2. Chill at least 2 hours. Just before serving, add shrimp.

Serves 8

Calories per serving:	132
Protein:	6 gm
Carbohydrate:	27 gm
Fat:	2 gm=13%

GARBANZO BEAN SOUP

1	acorn squash, halved and seeded
1 3/4 cups	water
1	28-oz can crushed tomatoes, undrained
1 med	onion, chopped
1 med	carrot, chopped
1 med	stalk celery, chopped
1 tsp	beef-flavored bouillon granules
1/2 tsp	ground cumin
1/2 tsp	caraway seeds, crushed
1/4 tsp	red pepper
1	bay leaf
1	15 oz can garbanzo beans, drained
1 med	zucchini, cut into 1-inch slices

1. Peel acorn squash, and cut into 3/4-inch pieces.
2. Combine acorn squash and next 10 ingredients in a large Dutch oven; bring to a boil. Cover, reduce heat, and simmer 15 minutes.
3. Add garbanzo beans and zucchini; simmer 10 minutes or until zucchini is tender. Discard bay leaf.
4. Ladle into soup bowls to serve.

Serves 9

Calories per serving:	86
Protein:	3.5 gm
Carbohydrate:	17.7 gm
Fat:	0.9 gm=10%

CARROT AND PARSNIP CHOWDER

4 med	carrots, diced
3 med	parsnips, diced
1 med	onion, chopped
1 med	potato, peeled and diced
3 1/2 cups	water
1 tsp	chicken-flavored bouillon
3/4 tsp	dried whole dillweed or 1 Tbsp chopped fresh dill
1/8 tsp	pepper

1. Combine first 6 ingredients in a large saucepan; bring to a boil.
2. Cover; reduce heat, and simmer 40 minutes or until vegetables are very tender.
3. Place 2 cups vegetable mixture into container of a blender; add dillweed and pepper, and process until smooth.
4. Return puréed mixture to saucepan with remaining vegetable mixture, and cook over low heat until thoroughly heated. Ladle into individual soup bowls to serve.

Serves 4

Calories per serving:	146
Protein:	3.7 gm
Carbohydrate:	33.2 gm
Fat:	0.8 gm=6%

BEEF STEW

	non-stick cooking spray
2 lbs	lean boneless round steak
5 cups	water
1 med	onion, sliced
1 clove	garlic, minced
2 tsp	beef-flavored bouillon granules
1 tsp	steak sauce
1/2 tsp	salt
1/2 tsp	dried whole thyme
1	bay leaf
6 small	onions (about 1 1/2 lbs), quartered
5 med	carrots
4 med	potatoes, cubed
3	stalks celery
2 Tbsp	all-purpose flour
1/4 cup	water

1. Trim excess fat from steak; cut steak into 1-inch pieces.
2. Coat a large Dutch oven with cooking spray; place over medium heat until hot. Add beef; cook until browned.
3. Stir in next 8 ingredients. Cover, reduce heat, and simmer 1 hour.
4. Add quartered onions, carrots, potatoes, and celery; cover and cook over low heat 30 minutes or until tender.
5. Remove bay leaf.
6. Combine flour and 1/4 cup water; stir into stew. Bring to a boil; cook 1 minute, stirring constantly. Ladle into soup bowls to serve.

Serves 16

Calories per serving:	166
Protein:	19.8 gm
Carbohydrate:	13.7 gm
Fat:	3.3 gm=18%

LENTIL STEW

1 qt	water
1 cup	onion, chopped
1 cup	potato, diced
1 cup	carrot, chopped
1 cup	fresh mushrooms, sliced
1/2 cup	celery, chopped
1/2 cup	tomato, chopped
1/2 cup	dried lentils
1/4 cup	brown rice, uncooked
2	vegetable-flavored bouillon cubes
1/2 tsp	dried whole tarragon
1/2 tsp	dried whole oregano

1. Combine all ingredients in a large Dutch oven, and bring to a boil.
2. Cover, reduce heat to low, and simmer 1 1/2 hours. Ladle into soup bowls to serve.

Serves 4

Calories per serving:	195
Protein:	9.6 gm
Carbohydrate:	38.8 gm
Fat:	0.9 gm=4%

Chapter 15

Sauces

For Healthy Living

RANCH DRESSING

1 cup	buttermilk
1 Tbsp	prepared mustard
1 tsp	onion, minced
1/8 tsp	dried dill
1 tsp	dried parsley
1/2 tsp	black pepper
1/2 cup	low fat yogurt

1. Combine all ingredients in a jar. Cover tightly and shake until smooth.
2. Chill. Shake well before serving.

Yield: 1 1/2 cups=24 Tbsp

Calories per serving:	7
Protein:	Trace
Carbohydrate:	Trace
Fat:	Trace

LOW CALORIE ITALIAN DRESSING

1/2 cup	red wine vinegar
1/2 tsp	fruit juice concentrate
1/2 tsp	oregano
1/4 tsp	basil
1/4 tsp	tarragon
1/2 tsp	dry mustard
1/4 tsp	black pepper
1/2 tsp	garlic, minced
3/4 tsp	steak sauce
1/4 cup	bran
1/2 cup	vinegar

1. Combine all ingredients in blender and blend at top speed for 2 minutes.
2. Chill before serving.

Yield: 1 cup=16 Tbsp

Calories per serving:	4
Protein:	Trace
Carbohydrate:	1 gm
Fat:	Trace

RUSSIAN DRESSING

2 small	carrots, thinly sliced
1/2 cup	water
1/2 med	tomato
2 Tbsp	lemon juice
1/2 cup	red wine vinegar
1/3 cup	onion, finely chopped
1 tsp	paprika

1. Simmer carrots in water until tender.
2. Purée tomato in blender. Add cooked carrots and water; blend with remaining ingredients until smooth. Chill before serving.

Yield: 2 cups=32 Tbsp

Calories per serving:	8
Protein:	Trace
Carbohydrate:	1 gm
Fat:	Trace

CHEESE SAUCE

1 Tbsp	all-purpose flour
1 cup	skim milk
2 Tbsp	sharp cheddar cheese, grated
Dash	cayenne
Dash	dry mustard

1. Shake flour and skim milk together in a tightly covered jar until smooth.
2. Pour into saucepan and heat.
3. Add cheese. Stir until melted.
4. Remove from heat and add cayenne and mustard. Serve hot.

Yield: 1 cup=16 Tbsp

Calories per serving:	10
Protein:	Trace
Carbohydrate:	1 gm
Fat:	Trace

FOUR STAR SEAFOOD SAUCE

1 cup	tomato juice
1 tsp	horseradish
1 tsp	lemon juice
1/2 tsp	steak sauce
1/2 tsp	parsley, chopped

1. Cook tomato juice down to half its volume.
2. Stir in additional ingredients and serve.

Yield: 1/2 cup=8 Tbsp

Calories per serving:	6
Protein:	Trace
Carbohydrate:	1 gm
Fat:	Trace

SALSA

2 large	tomatoes, peeled and chopped
1	onion, chopped
1	4-oz can green chilies, diced
1/4 cup	lemon juice
1 clove	garlic, pressed

1. Combine all ingredients and store in refrigerator until ready to use. Use freely.

Yield: 2 1/2 cups=40 Tbsp

Calories per serving:	3
Protein:	Trace
Carbohydrate:	Trace
Fat:	Trace

SPICY TOMATO SAUCE

1 cup	tomato sauce
1 Tbsp	vinegar
1 Tbsp	prepared mustard
2 tsp	steak sauce
1/4 tsp	onion powder
Dash	hot sauce
1/4 tsp	garlic powder

1. Combine all ingredients and bring to a boil.
2. Turn heat down and simmer about 8 minutes. Serve.

Yield: 1 cup=16 Tbsp

Calories per serving:	7
Protein:	Trace
Carbohydrate:	1 gm
Fat:	Trace

BARBECUE SAUCE

3/4 cup	catsup
3/4 cup	water
2 Tbsp	red wine vinegar
1/4 tsp	black pepper
1 tsp	chili powder
1 tsp	paprika
1 1/2 Tbsp	steak sauce

1. Combine all ingredients and heat.
2. Use over chicken, baked potatoes, or as a seasoning.

Yield: 2 cups=8 Servings

Calories per serving:	25
Protein:	0 gm
Carbohydrate:	7 gm
Fat:	Trace

GOLDEN GRAVY

1 cup	yellow split peas
3 cups	water
1/2 tsp	salt

1. Combine all ingredients in a saucepan and cook over medium heat from 30 to 60 minutes or until split peas are tender.
2. Pour mixture into a blender and blend until smooth.
3. Return to saucepan. Adjust consistency with water or chicken bouillon if necessary. Season. Serve.

Yield: 4 cups=8 servings

Calories per serving:	87
Protein:	6 gm
Carbohydrate:	16 gm
Fat:	Trace

MUSHROOM ONION GRAVY

1 pkg	dry onion soup
2 cups	water
2 Tbsp	cornstarch
1	3-oz can mushrooms, sliced

1. Combine onion soup mix and water.
2. Whisk in cornstarch.
3. Add mushrooms.
4. Heat, stirring constantly, until thickened. Serve.

Yield: 2 cups=4 servings

Calories per serving:	28
Protein:	1 gm
Carbohydrate:	2 gm
Fat:	1/2 gm=16%

HOT DILL SAUCE

1 cup	water
1/3 cup	non-fat dry milk
3 Tbsp	cornstarch
1 Tbsp	prepared mustard
1/4 tsp	dill seed

1. Combine and beat all ingredients with an electric mixer until well-blended.
2. Cook over medium heat, stirring constantly, until thickened.

Serves 4

Calories per serving:	63
Protein:	4 gm
Carbohydrate:	9 gm
Fat:	1 gm=14%

BASIC BUTTER SPREAD

1/2 cup	low fat cottage cheese
2 Tbsp	non-fat dry milk
1/2 tsp	imitation butter flavor
Dash	yellow food coloring (optional)

1. Blend cottage cheese, non-fat dry milk, and butter flavor until smooth. Add food coloring, if desired.
2. Chill.

VARIATION:
Add one of the following:

3 Tbsp	well-drained crushed pineapple
1 tsp	grated orange rind
1 Tbsp	finely chopped parsley
1 tsp	finely chopped chives

Yield: 1/2 cup=8 Tbsp

Calories per serving:	14
Protein:	2 gm
Carbohydrate:	1 gm
Fat:	Trace

TARTAR SAUCE

1/2 cup	low fat yogurt
1/4 cup	carrot, finely chopped
1 Tbsp	dill pickle, finely chopped
1 tsp	onion, finely chopped
1 tsp	parsley, minced
1 tsp	pimento
1 tsp	lemon juice

1. Combine all ingredients. Chill and serve.

Yield: 12 Tbsp

Calories per serving:	7
Protein:	Trace
Carbohydrate:	1 gm
Fat:	Trace

CZECHOSLOVAKIAN DRESSING

1 cup	water
1/3 cup	non-fat dry milk
3 Tbsp	cornstarch
1 Tbsp	prepared mustard
1/4 tsp	dill seed

1. Combine all ingredients. Beat with an electric mixer.
2. Cook over medium heat, stirring constantly, until thickened. Serve hot.

Serves 4

Calories per serving:	63
Protein:	4 gm
Carbohydrate:	9 gm
Fat:	1 gm=14%

MUSTARD DRESSING

1 cup	low fat cottage cheese
1 tsp	vinegar
2 tsp	prepared mustard
4 Tbsp	skim milk

1. Blend in blender until smooth and creamy, about 3 minutes. Chill before serving.

Yield: 1 cup

Calories per serving:	9
Protein:	Trace
Carbohydrate:	1 gm
Fat:	Trace

Chapter 16

Vegetables
For Healthy Living

ZUCCHINI STACK

3 med	zucchini, peeled and sliced
1/4 cup	onion, chopped
1 lb	low fat cottage cheese
1 Tbsp	lemon juice
1/4 tsp	basil
1/4 cup	grated Parmesan cheese

1. Sauté zucchini and onion.
2. Whip cottage cheese, lemon juice, and basil in blender.
3. Alternate layers of zucchini and cottage cheese mixture in a 1 1/2-quart non-stick casserole dish.
4. Top with Parmesan cheese. Bake uncovered at 350° for 25-30 minutes. Serve hot.

Serves 6

Calories per serving:	98
Protein:	16 gm
Carbohydrate:	6 gm
Fat:	1 1/2 gm=14%

STUFFED SQUASH

1 1/2 cups	brown rice, cooked
1/2 cup	dried whole wheat bread crumbs
1 med	onion, finely chopped
2	egg white, slightly beaten
1/2 tsp	sage
2 tsp	parsley, snipped
1 tsp	black pepper
3	acorn squash

1. Combine all ingredients except squash.
2. Cut squash in half. Clean out seeds and discard.
3. Fill each squash half with rice mixture, heaping slightly.
4. Place squash into a non-stick casserole. Seal with aluminum foil. Bake at 350° for 1 hour or until squash is tender. Serve.

Serves 6

Calories per serving:	196
Protein:	6 gm
Carbohydrate:	45 gm
Fat:	Trace

PERFECTLY COOKED BROCCOLI

1 lb	fresh broccoli
2 Tbsp	onion, minced
1 clove	garlic, minced
1 Tbsp	lemon juice
To taste	salt

1. Trim broccoli to uniform size. Wash. Blanch for 8 minutes. Then submerge in ice-cold water for about 3 minutes and drain.
2. Sauté onion and garlic. Add broccoli. Cook gently until everything is crisp-tender, about 2 to 3 minutes. Add lemon juice. Season to taste. Serve.

Serves 4

Calories per serving:	35
Protein:	3 gm
Carbohydrate:	5 gm
Fat:	Trace

SIMPLE SCALLOPED CORN

1	17-oz can cream-style corn
1 cup	skim milk
1 cup	dried whole wheat bread crumbs
2 Tbsp	pimento, chopped
1/4 cup	onion, chopped
Dash	black pepper
2	egg whites, stiffly beaten

1. Combine corn and milk. Add 3/4 cup of crumbs, pimento, onion, and black pepper; mix well. Fold in stiffly beaten egg whites.
2. Pour into non-stick 1-quart baking dish.
3. Top with remaining 1/4 cup of bread crumbs. Bake at 350° for 45 minutes. Serve hot.

Serves 8

Calories per serving:	107
Protein:	5 gm
Carbohydrate:	21 gm
Fat:	Trace

EXTRA SPECIAL ASPARAGUS

1/4 cup	onion, diced
1	green pepper, chopped
1/2 cup	mushrooms, sliced
2	10 oz pkg asparagus spears, frozen
2 tsp	pimento, diced
2 tsp	parsley, chopped

1. Bring to a boil onion, green pepper, and mushrooms in a saucepan. Cover and simmer for 5 minutes. Drain.
2. Steam asparagus until tender, about 12-15 minutes.
3. Combine asparagus with onion mixture and garnish with pimento and parsley before serving.

Serves 6

Calories per serving:	29
Protein:	4 gm
Carbohydrate:	5 gm
Fat:	Trace

FAVORITE SLICED BEETS

1 can (1 lb)	sliced beets
1 Tbsp	cornstarch
Dash	black pepper
1/4 cup	red wine vinegar
2 tsp	sugar

1. Drain beets, reserving liquid. Add enough water to beet juice to make 2/3 cup liquid.
2. Combine cornstarch and pepper in saucepan. Add liquid and vinegar. Whisk until smooth.
3. Cook, stirring constantly, until mixture is thickened and comes to boil. Continue stirring and boiling for 1 minute.
4. Add sliced beets and sugar. Heat and serve.

Serves 5

Calories per serving:	44
Protein:	1 gm
Carbohydrate:	10 gm
Fat:	Trace

VEGETABLES ORIENTAL

2 cups	chicken stock
2 med	onions, chopped
3 cloves	garlic, minced
1/2 bunch	broccoli florets, chopped
1 large	carrot, chopped
1/2 lb	mushrooms, sliced
8 cups	brown rice, cooked
1/4 cup	mung bean sprouts
1/4 cup	alfalfa sprouts
1 Tbsp	soy sauce

1. Prepare all ingredients.
2. Heat wok or large non-stick skillet. Add chicken stock and sauté onion, garlic, broccoli, and carrots until crisp-tender.
3. Add mushrooms. Cook 2 to 3 minutes more.
4. Add rice; stir as it is reheated. Sprinkle sprouts and soy sauce over rice mixture and heat 3 minutes longer. Serve immediately.

Serves 12

Calories per serving:	181
Protein:	5 gm
Carbohydrate:	38 gm
Fat:	1 gm=5%

CAULIFLOWER-N-CHEESE

1 med	cauliflower
To taste	seasoning without salt
1 cup	Cheese Sauce (page 109)

1. Wash cauliflower well; cut off the outside leaves and core.
2. Separate into florets. Steam or cover with 1-inch boiling water and cook 10 minutes. Cook until crisp-tender.
3. Drain and season. Top with Cheese Sauce. Serve immediately.

Serves 4

Calories per serving:	64
Protein:	5 gm
Carbohydrate:	8 gm
Fat:	1 gm=14%

BROCCOLI SOUFFLÉ

2 cups	broccoli, chopped
1/2 cup	onion, chopped
1 1/2 oz	part-skim mozzarella cheese, shredded
1/2 cup	low fat cottage cheese
2	egg whites, stiffly beaten

1. Cook broccoli and onion together in steamer or small amount of water. Drain well. Put into casserole dish.
2. Mix mozzarella cheese into hot broccoli. Blend in cottage cheese; then fold in egg whites.
3. Sprinkle with paprika. Bake at 350° for 30 minutes.

Serves 5

Calories per serving:	100
Protein:	10 gm
Carbohydrate:	2 gm
Fat:	2 gm=18%

HERBED CARROTS

1 Tbsp	lemon juice
1/8 cup	water
2 tsp	powdered butter substitute
1/4 tsp	allspice
1 1/2 cups	carrots, sliced diagonally
1 Tbsp	parsley, minced

1. Combine lemon juice, water, and butter substitute in small pot. Bring to boil. Stir butter substitute until dissolved.
2. Add carrots. Bring to boil again, then reduce heat to medium low. Cook for 5-8 minutes. The width of slices and your own preference for crispness should be the determining factors. When done, there should be no water in pot, and there should be a thin glaze on carrots.
3. Toss with parsley and serve.

Serves 4

Calories per serving:	30
Protein:	Trace
Carbohydrate:	8 gm
Fat:	Trace

BROCCOLI WITH DILL SAUCE

1   10-oz pkg broccoli
1   recipe Hot Dill Sauce (page 116)

1. Cook broccoli. Do not overcook.
2. Prepare Hot Dill Sauce. Pour over broccoli and serve immediately.

Serves 4

Calories per serving:	83
Protein:	6 gm
Carbohydrate:	12 gm
Fat:	1 gm=11%

STUFFED CUCUMBERS

1	6 1/2 oz can tuna, water-packed
1 slice	wheat bread crumbs
1 med	stalk celery, chopped fine
1/4 cup	sweet red pepper, finely chopped
1	green onion, chopped fine
2 Tbsp	plain yogurt
1 Tbsp	parsley, minced
2 tsp	lemon juice
2 Tbsp	fat-free mayonnaise
1 1/2 tsp	olive oil
1 tsp	Dijon or spicy brown mustard
1/4 tsp	dried tarragon, crumbled
4 med	cucumbers, unwaxed

1. In a small bowl, mix all the ingredients but the cucumbers and set aside.
2. Halve each cucumber crosswise. Using an apple corer or small paring knife, carefully scoop out the centers, leaving shells about 1/4-inch thick. Stuff the tuna mixture into each hollowed-out cucumber half, wrap in plastic food wrap, and refrigerate at least 4 hours.
3. Cut the cucumbers into 1/2-inch slices. Makes 48 appetizers.

Serves 8

Calories per serving:	12
Protein:	1 gm
Carbohydrate:	1 gm
Fat:	0

SPINACH SQUARES

1 lb	fresh spinach, trimmed and chopped, or
1	10-oz pkg frozen chopped spinach, thawed
Pinch	ground nutmeg
Pinch	sugar
1 cup	low fat cottage cheese
2 tsp	flour
2 Tbsp	grated Parmesan cheese
1 large	egg yolk
1/8 tsp	black pepper
Pinch	cayenne pepper
2 large	egg whites

1. Preheat the oven to 400°. Line the bottom of an 8x8x2-inch baking pan with waxed paper or baking parchment and set aside.
2. Wash the spinach and place into heavy 12-inch skillet with just water that clings to the leaves. Set over moderate heat and sprinkle with the nutmeg and sugar; cook, uncovered, stirring occasionally, until the spinach is tender—about 5 minutes. Cool to room temperature.
3. Place the cottage cheese into a food processor or blender and whirl for 30 seconds. Add the flour, Parmesan cheese, egg yolk, black pepper, and cayenne pepper, and whirl 30 seconds longer or until well-blended. Transfer to a large bowl and mix in the cooled spinach.

4. In a medium-size bowl, beat the egg whites until they hold stiff peaks. Mix about 1/4 cup of the beaten whites into the spinach mixture, then, with a rubber spatula, gently fold in the rest. Transfer the mixture to the baking pan, smoothing the top with the spatula. Bake, uncovered, for 20 minutes or until set and golden.
5. Place the pan on a wire rack and cool for 5 minutes, then invert onto large platter. Cut into 4 pieces to serve as a first course, or into 1 1/2-inch squares to serve as a party finger food.

Serves 4

Calories per serving:	92
Protein:	13 gm
Carbohydrate:	6 gm
Fat:	2 gm=20%

VEGGIES ANTIPASTO

4 small	carrots, peeled and thinly sliced diagonally
1 small	zucchini, peeled and sliced into matchstick strips
1/4 lb	broccoli florets
6	baby red potatoes, quartered
1/3 lb	fresh green beans
1 clove	garlic, minced
1/4 cup	fresh lemon juice
1 Tbsp	olive oil
1/2 tsp	salt
1/4 tsp	black pepper

1. In a steamer rack over boiling water, steam vegetables one type at a time until crisp-tender; carrots, zucchini, and broccoli about 2 minutes each; potatoes and green beans about 6-10 minutes. As each vegetable is cooked, remove to large, shallow serving bowl.
2. While vegetables are steaming, in a small saucepan combine garlic, lemon juice, olive oil, salt, and pepper, and simmer 5-10 minutes. Pour sauce over cooked vegetables.

Serves 6

Calories per serving:	126
Protein:	3 gm
Carbohydrate:	24 gm
Fat:	2 gm=14%

STUFFED MUSHROOMS

1 lb	large mushrooms, whole
1	10 oz pkg frozen chopped spinach
2	cloves garlic, minced
2	egg whites, stiffly beaten
1/2 cup	dried whole wheat bread crumbs

1. Wash mushrooms and remove caps. Heat caps in microwave oven for 2 minutes or steam briefly. Mince mushroom stems.
2. Cook spinach according to package directions along with chopped mushroom stems. Drain and squeeze to eliminate excess water.
3. Combine spinach with garlic, egg whites, and bread crumbs.
4. Fill mushroom caps with the spinach mixture. Place caps into a non-stick pan and bake 10-15 minutes. Serve hot.

Serves 4

Calories per serving:	72
Protein:	6 gm
Carbohydrate:	7 gm
Fat:	Trace

GRILLED TOMATOES

3	large ripe tomatoes, halved
1/4 tsp	olive oil
1/2 tsp	powdered rosemary
1/4 tsp	salt
1/4 tsp	black pepper
3 cloves	garlic, slivered

1. Brush tomato halves with olive oil, then sprinkle with rosemary, salt, and pepper.
2. Divide slivered garlic among tomatoes, pushing each sliver all the way into the tomato. Grill herb side up 8-10 minutes.

Serves 6

Calories per serving:	16
Protein:	Trace
Carbohydrate:	3 gm
Fat:	Trace

VEGETABLE STIR-FRY

1/2 small head	cauliflower
1/2 lb	broccoli
1/2 cup plus 1 Tbsp	fresh lemon juice
4 tsp	water
1 cup	chicken broth
1/4 tsp	soy sauce
1 Tbsp	grated lemon rind
1 clove	garlic
2 Tbsp	cornstarch

1. Break cauliflower and broccoli into florets.
2. In a wok or heavy skillet, heat 1 Tbsp of the lemon juice and 2 tsp of the water.
3. Add cauliflower and stir-fry 3-4 minutes.
4. Add broccoli and stir-fry 2-3 minutes longer or just until cauliflower and broccoli are crisp-tender.
5. In a medium saucepan, combine chicken broth, remaining lemon juice, soy sauce, lemon rind, and garlic, and heat to boiling.
6. In a covered jar, shake together cornstarch and remaining 2 tsp of water.
7. Gradually add to broth, stirring constantly until thickened. Pass sauce with vegetables.

Serves 4

Calories per serving:	61
Protein:	4 gm
Carbohydrate:	12 gm
Fat:	Trace

STUFFED TOMATOES

4 large	ripe tomatoes
6 cups	fresh spinach leaves
1 tsp	hot sauce

1. Scoop pulp and seeds from tomatoes (reserve for soup). Drain tomatoes upside down for a few minutes.
2. In a non-stick skillet or in a microwave, steam spinach leaves, covered, 1-2 minutes or just until leaves begin to soften. (It is not necessary to use additional moisture in the spinach.) Set aside.
3. Arrange tomatoes in an 8x8x2-inch ovenproof casserole dish. Place under broiler 5-10 minutes or until tomatoes are hot.
4. Drizzle cavity of each tomato with 1/4 tsp of hot sauce. Fill each tomato with spinach. Serve at once.

VARIATION:
Just before serving, sprinkle with freshly grated Parmesan cheese.

Serves 4

Calories per serving:	42
Protein:	3 gm
Carbohydrate:	8 gm
Fat:	Trace

CORN AND GREEN PEPPERS

1/2 cup	onion, chopped
1/4 cup	green bell pepper, chopped
1 cup	corn kernel
1/2 cup	tomato, chopped
1/4 cup	water
1	bay leaf
1/8 tsp	thyme
1/8 tsp	black pepper, freshly ground

1. Put the onion and bell pepper into a heavy saucepan and cook over medium heat while stirring for 2 minutes.
2. Add the corn and continue cooking, stirring occasionally, for 2 more minutes.
3. Add tomato, water, and seasonings.
4. Simmer uncovered for 10 minutes, or until most of the liquid is evaporated.

Serves 2

Calories per serving:	91.8
Protein:	3.5 gm
Carbohydrate:	20.3 gm
Fat:	1 gm=10%

COUSCOUS WITH VEGETABLES

1/4 lb	carrots, scraped and cut into julienne strips (about 3/4 cup)
1/2 lb	fresh asparagus, trimmed and cut into 1-inch pieces (about 1 cup)
3/4 cup	zucchini, diagonally sliced
1 cup	fresh snow peas
1 tsp	unsalted margarine, melted
1/4 cup	golden raisins
1/2 tsp	curry powder
1/4 tsp	ground cinnamon
1/4 tsp	dried whole thyme
3/4 cup	water
2 tsp	unsalted margarine
1/4 tsp	salt
1 cup	couscous, uncooked

1. Cook carrots in boiling water in a medium saucepan 8 minutes or until crisp-tender; drain and transfer to a large bowl.
2. Cook asparagus in boiling water in saucepan 3 minutes or until crisp-tender; drain and transfer to bowl.
3. Cook zucchini in boiling water in saucepan 2 minutes or until crisp-tender; drain and transfer to bowl.
4. Cook snow peas in boiling water in saucepan 1 minute; drain and transfer to bowl.
5. Toss vegetables with 1 tsp margarine, raisins, curry powder, cinnamon, and thyme; set aside, and keep warm.
6. Bring 3/4 cup water, 2 tsp margarine, and salt to a boil in saucepan; remove from heat, and add couscous.

7. Toss couscous 3 minutes or until water is absorbed.
8. Arrange couscous on a platter, and top with vegetable mixture.

Serves 8

Calories per serving:	70
Protein:	2.4 gm
Carbohydrate:	13.7 gm
Fat:	1.1 gm=14%

BULGUR LEEKS

1	10 3/4-oz can chicken broth, undiluted
1/2 cup	onion, diced
1/2 cup	leek, diced
1/2 cup	celery, diced
1 1/3 cups	water
1 cup	bulgur wheat, uncooked
1/8 tsp	pepper

1. Combine first 4 ingredients in a 2-quart saucepan; cover and cook over medium heat 6 minutes.
2. Add water and bring to a boil.
3. Add bulgur. Cover, reduce heat, and simmer 20 minutes or until liquid is absorbed.
4. Season with pepper, and spoon into bowl.

Serves 6

Calories per serving:	120
Protein:	4.6 gm
Carbohydrate:	24.2 gm
Fat:	0.8 gm=6%

SMOTHERED SQUASH

1 1/2 cups	yellow squash, sliced
1/2 cup	onion, chopped
1/2 cup	water
1 clove	garlic, minced
1/8 tsp	chili powder
To taste	black pepper, freshly ground

1. Put all ingredients into a small saucepan, cover, and simmer for 15 to 20 minutes, or until the squash is very tender.

Serves 2

Calories per serving:	34.2
Protein:	1.5 gm
Carbohydrate:	7.5 gm
Fat:	Trace

TURNIPS AND GREENS

2 med	turnips with their tops
1/2 cup	water
1/4 cup	green onion, chopped
1 clove	garlic, minced
1/8 tsp	black pepper, freshly ground

1. Cut the tops off the turnips and carefully wash both the greens and the turnips.
2. Chop the greens and set them aside.
3. Peel the turnips and cut them into 1/2-inch cubes.
4. Put the cubes into a saucepan with water, green onion, garlic, and pepper.
5. Simmer for 10 minutes, or until the turnips are almost tender.
6. Add the turnip tops, cover, and simmer for another 10 minutes, or until they are tender.

Serves 2

Calories per serving:	18.7
Protein:	.89 gm
Carbohydrate:	4.6 gm
Fat:	Trace

STEAMED SPINACH

1 cup	onion, chopped
1 clove	garlic, minced
10 oz.	fresh spinach, stemmed
To taste	black pepper, freshly ground

1. Put the onion and garlic into a heavy saucepan and cook over high heat while stirring for 1-2 minutes, or until they begin to color.
2. Add the spinach and pepper. Cover the pan tightly and cook for a few more minutes, or until the spinach has collapsed and rendered its liquid.

Serves 2

Calories per serving:	60.4
Protein:	5.09 gm
Carbohydrate:	11.9 gm
Fat:	0.7 gm=10%

BOILED BRUSSELS SPROUTS

6 whole	black peppercorns
4 whole	cloves
4 whole	allspice
2	bay leaves
1/4 tsp	cayenne
1/4 tsp	thyme
1 qt	water
1 1/2 cups	brussels sprouts

1. Tie the peppercorns, cloves, and allspice in cheese-cloth. Add all spices and seasonings to the water and bring to a boil. Let the water boil for 2 minutes to draw the flavors from the seasonings.
2. Add the brussels sprouts and boil for 10 minutes or until they are tender.
3. Drain the sprouts and serve.

Serves 2

Calories per serving:	45
Protein:	4.5 gm
Carbohydrate:	10.1 gm
Fat:	Trace

Chapter 17

Pasta

For Healthy Living

BAKED RIGATONI WITH MOZZARELLA

1	1-lb can low sodium tomatoes, with juice
1 Tbsp	olive oil
1 med	yellow onion, chopped fine
1	8-oz can low sodium tomato sauce
3 cloves	garlic, minced
1/2 tsp	dried oregano, crumbled
1 tsp	dried basil, crumbled
1/4 tsp	fennel seeds, crushed
1/8 tsp	black pepper
8 oz	rigatoni or ziti noodles
1 cup	part-skim mozzarella cheese, shredded
2 Tbsp	grated Parmesan cheese

1. Preheat the oven to 375°. In blender or food processor, purée the tomatoes for 10 to 15 seconds. Set aside.
2. Heat the olive oil in a heavy 10-inch skillet over moderate heat for 1 minute; add the onion and cook, uncovered, until soft—about 5 minutes. Add the tomatoes, tomato sauce, garlic, oregano, basil, fennel seeds, and pepper; bring to a boil, reduce the heat to low, and simmer, uncovered, for 10 minutes, stirring often, until the sauce has thickened slightly.
3. Meanwhile, cook the rigatoni noodles according to the package directions, omitting the salt. Rinse with cold water, drain well, and place into an ungreased, shallow 1 1/2-quart casserole. Cover with the sauce and sprinkle with the mozzarella and Parmesan cheese.

4. Bake uncovered for 30 to 35 minutes or until bubbly and golden. Let stand for 5 minutes before serving.

Serves 4

Calories per serving:	376
Protein:	17 gm
Carbohydrate:	55 gm
Fat:	9 gm=22%

LINGUINE LORRAINE

8 oz	linguine or spaghetti
1 Tbsp	olive oil
1 small	yellow onion, chopped fine
2 cloves	garlic, minced
1 lb	fresh spinach, trimmed and chopped, or
1	10-oz pkg frozen chopped spinach, thawed and well-drained
1/2 cup	skim milk
1/2 cup	low sodium chicken broth
1/4 cup	grated Parmesan cheese
1/4 tsp	black pepper

1. In a large kettle, cook the linguine according to package directions, omitting the salt.
2. While the linguine is cooking, heat the olive oil in a small, heavy saucepan over moderate heat for 1 minute; add the onion and garlic, and cook, uncovered, until the onion is soft—about 5 minutes. Add the spinach, milk, chicken broth, cheese, and pepper. Bring the mixture to a boil; reduce the heat and simmer, uncovered, for 3 minutes or until the sauce thickens slightly.
3. Pour the sauce into a blender or food processor and whirl until the mixture is puréed. Pour the sauce back into the saucepan and reheat over moderate heat until the mixture starts to simmer—about 1 minute.
4. Drain the linguine and return it to the kettle. Add the spinach mixture and toss well with 2 forks to mix. Transfer to a heated platter and serve.

VARIATION:
Substitute 2 cups chopped broccoli florets or 1 10-oz package frozen broccoli, chopped, for the spinach. Purée in Step 3, as directed.

Serves 4

Calories per serving:	295
Protein:	12 gm
Carbohydrate:	48 gm
Fat:	6 gm=18%

SPAGHETTI WITH ASPARAGUS

2 Tbsp	pecans, chopped
8 oz	spaghetti
3/4 lb	asparagus, tough stems removed, or
1	10-oz pkg frozen asparagus, cut into 1 1/2-inch lengths
1 clove	garlic, crushed
1 Tbsp	unsalted margarine
1/4 lb	mushrooms, sliced thin
1 Tbsp	chives, minced fresh or freeze dried
2 tsp	lemon juice
1/4 tsp	salt
1/4 tsp	black pepper
3 Tbsp	plain low fat yogurt

1. Preheat the oven to 350°. Place the pecans on a baking sheet and toast until crisp and somewhat darker—about 7 minutes. Set aside.
2. Meanwhile, cook the spaghetti according to package directions, omitting the salt. Drain, reserving 1/4 cup of the cooking water. Rinse and set aside. At the same time, add the asparagus to a large saucepan of boiling unsalted water and cook until tender but crisp—about 2 minutes. Set aside.
3. Rub a heavy 12-inch skillet with the garlic, then melt the margarine in the skillet over moderate high heat. Add the mushrooms and cook, stirring frequently, for 5 minutes. Add the cooked spaghetti, asparagus, and reserved cooking water, along with the chives, lemon juice, salt, and pepper. Toss with 2 forks. Add the yogurt and pecans and cook, tossing, until heated thoroughly, 2-3 minutes longer.

Serves 4

Calories per serving:	285
Protein:	10 gm
Carbohydrate:	47 gm
Fat:	6 gm=19%

LINGUINE, CHEESE, AND TOMATO PIE

8 oz	linguine
1 Tbsp	olive oil
1 med	yellow onion, chopped fine
3 cloves	garlic, minced
1/4 cup	minced parsley
1 Tbsp	lemon juice
1 1/2 tsp	dried oregano, crumbled
1 tsp	dried basil, crumbled
1/4 tsp	pepper, white or black
1/2 cup	part-skim ricotta cheese
1 large	egg white
1/4 cup	grated Parmesan cheese
2 med	tomatoes, cored, thinly sliced
1/4 cup	part-skim mozzarella cheese, shredded

1. Preheat the oven to 375°. Lightly grease and flour an 8-inch springform pan and set aside.
2. Cook the linguine according to package directions, omitting the salt. Drain, rinse under cold running water, and drain again. Return to the cooking pot and set aside.
3. Meanwhile, heat the olive oil in a heavy 7-inch skillet over moderate heat for 1 minute. Add the onion and garlic and cook, uncovered, until the onion is soft—about 5 minutes. Add to the linguine along with the parsley, lemon juice, 1 tsp of the oregano, 1/2 tsp of the basil, and the pepper; toss well. In a small bowl, combine the ricotta cheese, egg white, 2 Tbsp of the

Parmesan cheese, and the remaining 1/2 tsp of the oregano and basil; add to the linguine and toss well.

4. Turn half the linguine-cheese mixture into the prepared pan and press lightly over the bottom. Arrange half the tomato slices on top and sprinkle with half the mozzarella cheese; repeat the layers, using the remaining linguine, tomatoes, and mozzarella. Sprinkle the remaining Parmesan cheese on top.

5. Cover with aluminum foil and bake for 40 minutes or until set; remove the foil and bake 5 minutes longer. Cool for 10 minutes, then gently loosen the pie around the edges with a thin-bladed knife, remove the springform pan sides, and cut the pie into 8 wedges.

Serves 4

Calories per serving:	353
Protein:	16 gm
Carbohydrate:	51 gm
Fat:	9 gm=23%

LASAGNA ROLLS

1 cup	spinach
2 Tbsp	grated Parmesan cheese
1 cup	low fat cottage cheese
8 oz	whole wheat lasagna noodles
2 cups	Spicy Tomato Sauce (page 112)

1. Cook spinach; drain off all excess water. Stir in cheeses. Set aside.
2. Cook lasagna noodles.
3. Spread spinach mixture evenly along the entire length of each noodle. Roll up noodle and place on its side in a non-stick 8x8-inch casserole dish. Do not let noodles touch.
4. Cover lasagna with Spicy Tomato Sauce. Bake at 350° for 20 minutes. Serve hot.

Serves 4

Calories per serving:	215
Protein:	18 gm
Carbohydrate:	23 gm
Fat:	3 gm=13%

NOODLES ALFREDO

8 oz	broad egg noodles
1/4 cup	part-skim ricotta cheese
1/4 cup	plain low fat yogurt
1/4 cup	Parmesan cheese
1 Tbsp	unsalted margarine
1/4 tsp	black pepper

1. Cook the noodles according to package directions, omitting the salt. Drain well and return to the cooking pot.
2. Add the ricotta cheese, yogurt, Parmesan cheese, margarine, and pepper, and toss well to mix. Transfer to a warm platter and serve with a cooked green vegetable.

VARIATIONS:

Noodles with Mushrooms—Melt the margarine in a heavy 10-inch skillet over moderate heat. Add 1 1/2 cups sliced mushrooms and cook, stirring, for 3 to 5 minutes. Toss the remaining ingredients.

Noodles with Onion and Garlic—Melt the margarine in a heavy 7-inch skillet over moderate heat. Add 1 large yellow onion, sliced, and 1 clove garlic, minced. Cook uncovered, until the onion is soft—about 5 minutes. Toss with the noodles and the remaining ingredients.

Serves 4

Calories per serving:	299
Protein:	12 gm
Carbohydrate:	43 gm
Fat:	8 gm=24%

159

QUICHE

	non-stick cooking spray
1/2 cup	long grain rice
1 cup	Swiss cheese, shredded
3 large	egg whites
1 med	yellow onion, sliced thin
1 med	carrot, peeled and grated
1 med	zucchini, grated
1 cup	low sodium chicken broth
1/4 tsp	dried marjoram, crumbled
1 large	egg
1 cup	skim milk
1/4 tsp	black pepper

1. Cook the rice according to package directions, omitting salt.
2. Preheat the oven to 350°. Coat a 9-inch pie pan with the cooking spray and set aside. In a medium-size bowl, mix together the rice, 2 Tbsp of the cheese, and 1 egg white. With moistened hands, press the mixture over the bottom and sides of the pie pan. Bake, uncovered, for 5 minutes. Remove and cool upright on a wire rack while you prepare the filling.
3. In a medium-size saucepan, cook the onion, carrot, zucchini, chicken broth, and marjoram, uncovered, over moderate heat for 15 minutes. Increase the heat to high and cook, stirring, until all the liquid has evaporated and the vegetables are almost glazed—about 5 minutes. Transfer to a medium-size, heatproof bowl and cool to room temperature—about 20 minutes.
4. Lightly beat together the remaining egg whites and

the egg; mix into the cooled vegetables along with the milk, pepper, and remaining cheese. Pour the mixture into the pie shell and bake, uncovered, until the filling is puffed and set—about 20 minutes. Remove and cool for 15 minutes before serving.

Serves 10 as a first course or
Serves 4 as a main meal

Calories per serving:	127
Protein:	7 gm
Carbohydrate:	15 gm
Fat:	4 gm=28%

PASTA MCBARRON

1/4 cup	olive oil
2 Tbsp	balsamic vinegar
3 cloves	garlic
2 oz	fresh basil
1 tsp	salt
1/4 tsp	black pepper
1 lb	mostaccioli or other tube-shaped pasta, cooked *al dente*
1 1/2 lbs	ripe tomatoes, cubed
2 cups	Calamata olives, pitted and halved

1. In a blender or food processor, combine olive oil, vinegar, and garlic. Add 1/2 of the basil and whirl 1 minute. Add salt and pepper.
2. Pour over mostaccioli while pasta is still warm.
3. Add tomatoes and olives; toss. Garnish with remaining whole basil leaves.

Serves 8

Calories per serving:	167
Protein:	5 gm
Carbohydrate:	27 gm
Fat:	5 gm=27%

MOZZARELLA PASTA

1 lb	fresh, ripe tomatoes
6 cups	fresh basil
1 Tbsp	olive oil
1/2 tsp	salt
1/4 tsp	black pepper
1 lb	ziti or tube-shaped pasta, cooked
1 1/2 cups	part-skim mozzarella cheese, grated

1. Plunge tomatoes into boiling water for 1-2 minutes to soften skins, then into ice water; peel and coarsely chop. Coarsely chop 4 cups of the basil leaves; reserve remaining whole leaves for garnish.
2. In a non-stick skillet, heat olive oil and add tomatoes. Bring to a boil. Reduce heat to simmer and add chopped basil, salt, and pepper.
3. While pasta is still warm, toss with sauce and mozzarella. Turn pasta over and over to mix ingredients and melt cheese. Garnish with remaining 2 cups of basil.

Serves 8

Calories per serving:	365
Protein:	19 gm
Carbohydrate:	51 gm
Fat:	10 gm=24%

163

PENNE AND OLIVES

1 Tbsp	olive oil
1 cup	white onion, chopped
5 cloves	garlic, minced
1	28-oz can plum tomatoes, coarsely chopped
1/2 tsp	red pepper, crushed
1/2 tsp	salt
1 cup	Calamato olives, chopped
2 oz	anchovy fillets, chopped
3 Tbsp	drained capers
1 lb	penne or other tube-shaped pasta, cooked *al dente*
1/3 cup	Parmesan cheese

1. In a non-stick skillet, heat olive oil. Add onions and garlic, and sauté 6-8 minutes. Pour into a small stockpot.
2. Add tomatoes, crushed red pepper, and salt. Heat to just boiling; reduce heat and simmer 10 minutes.
3. Add olives, anchovies, and capers. Serve over pasta. Sprinkle with Parmesan cheese.

Serves 8

Calories per serving:	309
Protein:	13 gm
Carbohydrate:	49 gm
Fat:	8 gm=23%

TOMATO-MACARONI WITH CHICK PEAS

1 Tbsp	olive oil
1 clove	garlic, minced
1	1 lb can low sodium tomatoes, chopped (reserve liquid)
2 Tbsp	parsley, minced
1/2 tsp	dried basil, crumbled
1/2 tsp	oregano, crumbled
1/4 tsp	black pepper
1 cup	chick peas, cooked and drained
8 oz	elbow macaroni or ditalini

1. Heat the olive oil in a medium-size heavy saucepan, over moderate heat for 30 seconds; add the garlic and cook, stirring, for 30 seconds. Mix in the tomatoes, parsley, basil, oregano, and pepper; bring to a boil; lower the heat so that the mixture bubbles gently, then simmer, uncovered, for 10 minutes or until thickened.
2. Stir in the chick peas and simmer, uncovered, 10 minutes longer.
3. Meanwhile, cook the macaroni according to package directions, omitting the salt; drain well and transfer to a heated bowl. Pour the chick pea mixture over noodles and toss well.

Serves 4

Calories per serving:	339
Protein:	12 gm
Carbohydrate:	61 gm

165

RIGATONI WITH CURRIED VEGETABLES

1/2	16-oz pkg rigatoni or other tubular pasta
1 1/3 cups	green onion, chopped
1 med	carrot, scraped and coarsely grated
1 med	green pepper, seeded and cut into julienne strips
1 med	zucchini, coarsely grated
1/2 cup	water
1/2 tsp	chicken bouillon granules
2 cups	cauliflower florets
1 cup	broccoli florets
2 tsp	curry powder
3/4 cup	plain low fat yogurt
1/4 cup	sour cream
2 Tbsp	fresh parsley or coriander, minced
1 Tbsp	lemon juice

1. Cook rigatoni according to package directions, omitting salt; drain well. Set aside and keep warm.
2. Combine green onion, carrot, green pepper, zucchini, water, and bouillon granules in a Dutch oven; bring to a boil.
3. Reduce heat, and cook, uncovered, 5 minutes, stirring occasionally. Add cauliflower and broccoli; simmer 5 minutes or until tender.
4. Stir in curry powder; simmer 2 minutes.

5. Stir in remaining ingredients, and cook over medium-low heat until thoroughly heated, stirring occasionally. (Do not boil.)
6. Serve over warm pasta.

Serves 8

Calories per serving:	160
Protein:	6.4 gm
Carbohydrate:	28.8 gm
Fat:	2.5 gm=14%

SPAGHETTI WITH SPRING VEGETABLES

	non-stick cooking spray
1	16 oz pkg spaghetti
1/4 lb	fresh green beans
1 med	onion, thinly sliced
1 clove	garlic, minced
1 med	carrot, scraped and coarsely grated
1 med	red or green pepper, seeded and cut into julienne strips
1/2 cup	water
1/2 tsp	chicken-flavored bouillon granules
1/4 lb	fresh asparagus, cut into 3/4-inch pieces
1/2 cup	fresh English peas
1/2 cup	plain low fat yogurt
1/2 cup	sour cream
2 Tbsp	lemon juice
1/3 cup	fresh parsley, minced
1 Tbsp	chives, minced
1/4 tsp	dried whole tarragon or
1 Tbsp	fresh tarragon, minced
1/4 tsp	dried whole basil or
1 Tbsp	fresh basil, minced
1/8 tsp	pepper

1. Cook spaghetti according to package directions, omitting salt; drain well. Set aside, and keep warm.
2. Remove strings from beans and cut into 3/4-inch pieces; set aside.
3. Coat a large Dutch oven with cooking spray; place

over medium heat until hot. Add onion and garlic, and sauté 5 minutes or until tender.

4. Add carrot and red or green pepper; cook 2 minutes, stirring constantly

5. Add water, bouillon granules, asparagus, peas, and green beans; cook, covered, 8 minutes or until vegetables are crisp-tender.

6. Add remaining ingredients; cook until thoroughly heated, stirring frequently. (Do not allow sauce to boil.)

7. Serve over warm pasta.

Serves 16

Calories per serving:	140
Protein:	5 gm
Carbohydrate:	25.4 gm
Fat:	2.1 gm=14%

VERMICELLI

	non-stick cooking spray
16 oz	vermicelli
2 cloves	garlic, minced
1 med	onion, thinly sliced
5 med	tomatoes, peeled and chopped
8 oz	unsalted tomato sauce
1 Tbsp	dried whole basil, or
1/4 cup	fresh basil, minced
1/8 tsp	pepper
2 Tbsp	grated Parmesan cheese

1. Cook vermicelli according to package directions, omitting salt; drain and set aside.
2. Coat a Dutch oven with cooking spray; place over medium heat until hot.
3. Add garlic and onion; sauté 5 minutes or until tender.
4. Stir in tomato, tomato sauce, basil, and pepper; simmer 15 minutes.
5. Stir in vermicelli, and cook over low heat until thoroughly heated, stirring occasionally.
6. Transfer to a large platter, and sprinkle with Parmesan cheese to serve.

Serves 8

Calories per serving:	143
Protein:	5.4 gm
Carbohydrate:	28.5 gm
Fat:	0.9 gm=6%

LINGUINE IN CLAM SAUCE

	non-stick cooking spray
1 cup	chopped onion
1 clove	garlic, minced
6 oz	tomato paste
1 cup	tomato, diced
1 tsp	dried whole basil
1 tsp	dried whole oregano
1/8 tsp	pepper
1	bay leaf
1/2 cup	dry red wine
2	6 1/2 oz cans minced clams, rinsed and drained
8 oz	linguine

1. Coat a medium skillet with cooking spray, and place over low heat until hot. Add onion and garlic; sauté 5 minutes. Add next 7 ingredients.
2. Bring to a boil. Cover, reduce heat, and simmer 30 minutes. Add clams; cover and simmer 30 minutes.
3. Discard bay leaf. Cook linguine according to package directions, omitting salt and fat; drain. Combine red clam sauce and linguine in a large bowl, tossing gently. Serve immediately.

Serves 4

Calories per serving:	311
Protein:	15.4 gm
Carbohydrate:	58.4 gm
Fat:	2.2 gm=6%

ZITI SALAD WITH AVOCADO SAUCE

1	16-oz pkg ziti
3/4 cup	plain non-fat yogurt
1 med	green chile, seeded and minced
1/4 cup	fresh parsley or coriander, minced
3 Tbsp	lemon juice
1 clove	garlic, minced
1/4 tsp	salt
1/8 tsp	pepper
1 med	avocado, cubed and divided
1 med	red or green pepper, seeded and chopped
2 med	tomatoes, seeded and chopped
1/2 cup	green onion, minced

1. Cook ziti according to package directions, omitting salt; drain and set aside.
2. Combine yogurt, chile pepper, parsley, lemon juice, garlic, salt, pepper, and 1/2 cup avocado in container of a blender; process until puréed.
3. Combine avocado sauce and ziti in a large bowl; add remaining avocado, red or green pepper, tomato, and green onion; toss gently.
4. Cover and chill 1 to 2 hours.

Serves 8

Calories per serving:	278
Protein:	9.3 gm
Carbohydrate:	49.6 gm
Fat:	5 gm=16%

BAKED MACARONI AND CHEESE

3 Tbsp	cornstarch
3 cups	skim milk
1 cup	sharp cheddar cheese, shredded
4 Tbsp	grated Parmesan cheese
2 Tbsp	onion, grated
3/4 tsp	dry mustard
1/4 tsp	each, salt and pepper
16 oz	cooked macaroni or bow tie pasta
1/2 cup	low fat cottage cheese
1/4 tsp	paprika

1. Combine cornstarch and milk in a Dutch oven; bring to a boil, reduce heat, and cook, stirring constantly with a wire whisk, 5 minutes, or until slightly thickened; remove from heat.
2. Add cheddar cheese, 3 Tbsp grated Parmesan cheese onion, mustard, salt, pepper, cooked macaroni, and cottage cheese to Dutch oven, mixing well.
3. Spoon mixture into a 13x9x2-inch baking dish coated with cooking spray. Sprinkle with 1 Tbsp Parmesan cheese and paprika. Bake at 350° for 30 minutes.

Serves 8

Calories per serving:	337
Protein:	16.9 gm
Carbohydrate:	51 gm
Fat:	6.7 gm=18%

VEGETABLE LASAGNA

	non-stick cooking spray
2 Tbsp	onion, chopped
1 clove	garlic, minced
1 tsp	olive oil
1 1/2 cups	tomato, peeled and diced
2 cups	eggplant, peeled and diced
1/2 cup	green pepper, chopped
1 med	zucchini, diced
1/4 lb	fresh mushrooms, chopped
1 tsp	dried whole oregano
1	bay leaf
1/4 tsp	salt
1/4 tsp	pepper
6	lasagna noodles, uncooked
1/8 tsp	salt
2	eggs, beaten
1 cup	low fat cottage cheese
1 Tbsp	fresh parsley, chopped
1/2 cup	mozzarella cheese, shredded
1 Tbsp	grated Parmesan cheese

1. Sauté onion and garlic in oil in a large skillet. Stir in next 9 ingredients.
2. Cover, reduce heat, and simmer 10 minutes. Remove bay leaf.
3. Cook lasagna according to package directions, reducing salt to 1/8 tsp. Drain noodles, and cut in half crosswise; set aside.
4. Coat an 8-inch-square baking dish with cooking spray. Place 4 noodle halves into dish.

5. Spoon half of cottage cheese mixture over noodles.
6. Spread half of vegetable mixture over cottage cheese mixture; sprinkle with half of mozzarella cheese.
7. Repeat layers, ending with noodles.
8. Cover and bake at 350° for 20 minutes.
9. Sprinkle with Parmesan cheese; cover and bake 5 minutes.

Serves 6

Calories per serving:	224
Protein:	14.4 gm
Carbohydrate:	28.4 gm
Fat:	6.3 gm=25%

FLAVOR WITHOUT FAT

Chapter 18

Potatoes

For Healthy Living

WHIPPED POTATOES

3 small	potatoes, peeled and quartered
1/4 cup	low fat cottage cheese
1/4 cup	skim milk
To taste	white pepper
1 Tbsp	Parmesan cheese
Garnish	chives, snipped

1. Boil potatoes in water until fork-tender, about 20 minutes. Drain well, making sure potatoes are completely dry.
2. Mash potatoes with a potato masher; transfer to electric mixer. Set aside.
3. In a blender, combine cottage cheese and skim milk until smooth. Add mixture to potatoes and whip until fluffy. Season to taste with white pepper.
4. Transfer whipped potatoes to shallow baking pan. Smooth top of potatoes and sprinkle evenly with Parmesan cheese.
5. Brown under broiler until golden. Sprinkle fresh chives on top of potatoes as garnish.

Serves 6

Calories per serving:	70
Protein:	2 gm
Carbohydrate:	14 gm
Fat:	Trace

ITALIAN STUFFED POTATOES

2	5 oz potatoes, baked
1 1/2 oz	part-skim mozzarella cheese, grated
1/2 cup	vegetables, steamed
1/4 tsp	basil
1/8 tsp	oregano
Dash	red pepper flakes

1. Add basil, oregano, and red pepper flakes to steamed vegetables; mix well.
2. Cut baked potato in half lengthwise and fluff with fork. Add vegetable mixture and sprinkle grated cheese on top.
3. Bake in oven at 350° until cheese melts.

Serves 2

Calories per serving:	170
Protein:	5 gm
Carbohydrate:	28 gm
Fat:	4 gm=21%

SWEET, SWEET POTATOES

1 lb	sweet potatoes
Pinch	cinnamon
Pinch	nutmeg
Pinch	allspice
1/4 cup	pineapple juice and
1 Tbsp	chopped pineapple, or
1/2 cup	orange juice
1/2 tsp	orange rind, grated

1. Boil sweet potatoes until tender. Remove skins.
2. Mash sweet potato pulp. Add spices and juice. Whip until fluffy.
3. Add fruit or rind and stir together.
4. Place into a 1-quart non-stick baking dish. Bake at 350° until thoroughly heated. Serve.

Serves 6

Calories per serving:	72
Protein:	1 gm
Carbohydrate:	16 gm
Fat:	Trace

SCALLOPED POTATOES

2 tsp	powdered butter substitute
2 Tbsp	whole wheat flour
1/4 tsp	black pepper
6	potatoes, sliced
1	onion, sliced
2 cups	skim milk

1. Combine butter substitute, flour, and pepper.
2. Layer potatoes and onions with flour mixture in a non-stick casserole dish.
3. Pour heated skim milk over potato layers.
4. Cover and bake at 350° for 1 1/2 hours. Serve hot.

Serves 6

Calories per serving:	131
Protein:	5 gm
Carbohydrate:	28 gm
Fat:	Trace

FRENCH FRIES

4	potatoes
1 Tbsp	barbecue sauce, or recipe on page 113
2 Tbsp	apple juice
1 tsp	seasoned salt

1. Boil potatoes in skins until tender.
2. Remove from water and chill.
3. Peel and slice into french fries or leave skins on and cut lengthwise into 8 wedges.
4. Place into a bowl and toss with 1 Tbsp barbecue sauce and seasoned salt.
5. Bake at 400° for 10 to 15 minutes on a non-stick baking sheet. Turn with spatula and continue baking for 10 to 15 minutes longer. Serve hot.

Serves 4

Calories per serving:	98
Protein:	3 gm
Carbohydrate:	20 gm
Fat:	Trace

POTATO BALLS

1/2 Tbsp	prepared mustard
2 drops	hot sauce
2 tsp	powdered butter substitute
3 cups	mashed potatoes
2	egg whites, stiffly beaten
1/2 cup	evaporated milk
1 cup	cornflake crumbs

1. Add mustard, hot sauce, and butter substitute to mashed potatoes and beat.
2. Fold in stiffly beaten egg whites.
3. Let cool briefly. Shape into 8 to 12 potato balls.
4. About 15 minutes before serving, brush potato balls with evaporated milk and roll in crumbs.
5. Bake at 425° for 5 to 6 minutes on a non-stick baking sheet. Turn with spatula and continue baking for 10 to 15 minutes longer. Serve hot.

Serves 4

Calories per serving:	98
Protein:	3 gm
Carbohydrate:	20 gm
Fat:	Trace

HASH BROWNS

4	potatoes, boiled
1	onion, chopped
1/2 cup	chicken bouillon
To taste	seasoning without salt

1. Shred boiled potatoes (preferably with skins on). Combine with chopped onion.
2. Cook in a heated non-stick pan using chicken bouillon instead of oil.
3. Season. Turn potatoes often, until golden brown. Serve.

Serves 4

Calories per serving:	91
Protein:	3 gm
Carbohydrate:	21 gm
Fat:	Trace

POTATO BROCCOLI CASSEROLE

4	small potatoes
1/4 cup	skim milk
2 tsp	powdered butter substitute
1	10 oz pkg frozen chopped broccoli
1/4 cup	cheddar cheese

1. Cook, drain, and mash potatoes with milk and butter substitute.
2. Cook broccoli according to package directions. Drain well. Fold into mashed potatoes.
3. Put into non-stick pan. Sprinkle with cheese.
4. Bake at 350° for 15 minutes or until cheese melts. Serve hot.

Serves 4

Calories per serving:	142
Protein:	7 gm
Carbohydrate:	23 gm
Fat:	2.4 gm=15%

CREAMED PEAS AND NEW POTATOES

10	new potatoes
1	10-oz pkg frozen peas or
1 lb	fresh peas
12	pearl onions, or
3 Tbsp	green onions, sliced
1 tsp	powdered butter substitute
1 1/2 Tbsp	cornstarch
1 cup	skim milk

1. Peel potatoes. Cover with water. Boil and cook until tender. Drain.
2. Cook peas and onions together until tender. Drain.
3. While vegetables are cooking, mix butter substitute, cornstarch, and milk together until smooth. Heat until thickened, stirring constantly.
4. Pour sauce over combined hot vegetables. Serve immediately.

Serves 6

Calories per serving:	102
Protein:	5 gm
Carbohydrate:	20 gm
Fat:	4.6 gm=4%

POTATO PUFFS

8 small	new potatoes (about 1/2 lb)
1/2 cup	low fat cottage cheese
2 Tbsp	parsley, minced
2 Tbsp	chives
2 Tbsp	fresh dill, snipped, or
1 tsp	dill weed
1/4 tsp	black pepper
8 small	sprigs dill or parsley (optional)

1. In a medium-size heavy saucepan over moderately high heat, bring to a boil enough unsalted water to cover the potatoes, reduce the heat to low, cover, and cook until tender—about 15 minutes. Drain.
2. Meanwhile, place the cottage cheese into a blender or food processor and whirl for 15 seconds or until smooth. Transfer to a small bowl and stir in the parsley, chives, snipped dill, and pepper.
3. When the potatoes are cool enough to handle, slice about 1/4 inch off the top of each. With a small spoon or melon baller, remove 1 or 2 scoops of potato, being careful not to break the skin. Fill the potatoes with the cheese mixture and garnish, if you like, with the dill or parsley sprigs.

Serves 4

Calories per serving:	34
Protein:	2 gm
Carbohydrate:	6 gm
Fat:	0

POTATOES AND TOMATOES

1/3 cup	beef consommé
2 Tbsp	dry white wine
1 tsp	chervil
1 Tbsp	parsley, chopped
1 Tbsp	olive oil
1/2 tsp	salt
1/4 tsp	black pepper
1 1/2 lbs	tiny red potatoes, cooked and halved
1/4 lb	fresh mushrooms, cooked and sliced, or
1	8-oz can mushroom stems and pieces, drained
1 large	tomato, diced

1. In a small bowl, combine consommé, white wine, chervil, parsley, olive oil, salt, and pepper. Pour over potatoes while potatoes are still warm.
2. Arrange in a low salad bowl. Toss with mushrooms and tomatoes.
3. Thoroughly drain excess marinade. Serve hot or cold.

Serves 8

Calories per serving:	100
Protein:	2 gm
Carbohydrate:	18 gm
Fat:	2 gm=18%

RED POTATO ROAST

1 lb	tiny red potatoes, halved
1/4 cup	fresh lemon juice
1 Tbsp	olive oil
1/2 tsp	salt
1/4 tsp	black pepper

1. In a 13x9x2-inch ovenproof casserole dish, arrange potatoes. Combine lemon juice, olive oil, salt, and pepper; pour over potatoes.
2. Roast in a 350° oven 30-40 minutes or until potatoes are tender, turning 3-4 times to baste.

Serves 4

Calories per serving:	157
Protein:	2 gm
Carbohydrate:	30 gm
Fat:	3 gm=17%

GARLIC POTATOES

1 lb	tiny red potatoes, halved
1	head of garlic, cloves separated but not peeled
2 Tbsp	olive oil
1/2 tsp	salt
1/4 tsp	black pepper

1. In a 9x13x2-inch ovenproof casserole dish, arrange potatoes in a single layer. Tuck garlic cloves among potatoes. Drizzle with olive oil, salt, and pepper.
2. Bake at 350° 30-40 minutes or until potatoes are tender and garlic is soft.
3. Squeeze garlic from peels on potatoes. Toss potatoes with pan drippings.

Serves 8

Calories per serving:	92
Protein:	1 gm
Carbohydrate:	16 gm
Fat:	3 gm=29%

Chapter 19

Chicken

For Healthy Living

MUSHROOM CHICKEN

	non-stick cooking spray
1/2 lb	mushrooms, chopped fine
3	green onions, chopped fine
3 cloves	garlic, minced
1/4 tsp	dried thyme
1/4 tsp	marjoram, crumbled
3 Tbsp	dry red wine
1/4 cup	low sodium chicken broth
2 tsp	lemon juice
1 lb	chicken breasts, skinned, boned and halved
4	thin slices reduced sodium ham

1. Set a heavy non-stick 7-inch skillet over low heat about 30 seconds. Add the mushrooms, green onions, and garlic; cover and cook for 10 minutes or until the mushrooms have released their juices. Mix in the thyme and marjoram.

2. Raise the heat to moderate, add the wine, and cook uncovered, for 5 minutes. Add the chicken broth and cook 5 minutes longer or until almost all the liquid has evaporated. Transfer the mushroom mixture to a bowl. When the mixture has cooled slightly, stir in the lemon juice.

3. Preheat the oven to 350°. Lightly coat 4 sheets of aluminum foil, each 10 inches long, with the spray. Lay 1 piece of the chicken on each piece of foil, spoon on 1/4 of the mushroom mixture, and top with a ham slice. Fold the foil over and crimp tightly to seal.

4. Place packets on a baking sheet and bake for 17-20 minutes or until the chicken is done.

Serves 4

Calories per serving: 183
Protein: 33 gm
Carbohydrate: 5 gm
Fat: 3 gm=15%

LEMON CAPER CHICKEN

1/4 cup	flour
1/4 tsp	black pepper
1/2 tsp	paprika
1 lb	chicken breast, skinned and boned, halved and pounded to 1/4-inch thickness
5 tsp	olive oil
1/4 cup	low sodium chicken broth
2 Tbsp	lemon juice
2 Tbsp	capers, drained

1. On a plate, combine the flour, pepper, and paprika. Press the chicken breasts into the mixture, coating them all over and shaking off any excess.
2. In a heavy 10-inch skillet, heat the olive oil over moderately high heat for 1 minute. Add the breasts and cook about 3 minutes on each side. Transfer the breasts to a heated platter.
3. Add the chicken broth to the skillet, scraping up any browned bits on the bottom. Stir in the lemon juice and capers and heat through. Pour the sauce over the breasts and serve hot.

Serves 4

Calories per serving:	208
Protein:	27 gm
Carbohydrate:	7 gm
Fat:	7 gm=30%

DIJON CHICKEN

2	whole chicken breasts, halved and skinned
2 Tbsp	Dijon or spicy mustard
1 tsp	lemon juice
1/4 tsp	black pepper
2	green onions, chopped
1/2 cup	soft white bread crumbs (1 slice)

1. Preheat the broiler and lightly grease the rack. Broil the chicken breasts 5-6 inches from the heat for 5 minutes; turn and broil 5 minutes longer.
2. Meanwhile, combine the mustard, lemon juice, pepper, and green onion. Coat the broiled chicken breasts all over with the mixture, place them back on the broiler rack, and sprinkle lightly with half of the bread crumbs. Broil for 2 minutes or until the crumbs are brown.
3. Turn the breasts, sprinkle with the remaining crumbs, and brown about 2 minutes longer or until the meat is no longer pink when cut at the center.

Serves 4

Calories per serving:	152
Protein:	27 gm
Carbohydrate:	5 gm
Fat:	2 gm=12%

CREOLE CHICKEN

2 Tbsp	unsalted margarine
1 med	yellow onion, chopped
1 med	sweet green pepper—cored, seeded, and diced
1 large	stalk celery, chopped
2 cloves	garlic, minced
2	whole chicken breasts, halved and skinned
1 tsp	paprika
1/4 tsp	cayenne pepper
1 can (1 lb)	low sodium stewed tomatoes
1 tsp	dried rosemary, crumbled
1/2 tsp	dried marjoram, crumbled
1	bay leaf
1 Tbsp	flour
1/4 cup	low sodium chicken broth or water

1. In a heavy 12-inch skillet, melt 1 Tbsp of the margarine over moderate heat. Add the onion, green pepper, celery, and garlic; cook, uncovered, until the onion is soft—about 5 minutes. Transfer to a small dish.
2. Raise the heat under the skillet to moderately high and add the remaining margarine. While it melts, sprinkle the paprika and cayenne pepper all over the chicken breasts. Add the chicken to the skillet and cook about 5 minutes, turning occasionally.
3. Add half of the cooked vegetables to the skillet along with the tomatoes, rosemary, marjoram, and bay leaf; reduce the heat, cover, and simmer for 20 minutes or until the chicken is fork-tender.

4. Mix the flour into the broth or water and whisk into the skillet. Cook, stirring constantly, until the sauce has thickened—about 3 minutes. Return the remaining vegetables to the skillet and heat for 3 minutes. Discard the bay leaf. Serve with fluffy boiled rice.

Tip:
Ounce for ounce, dark meat has twice the fat content of white meat.

Serves 4

Calories per serving:	276
Protein:	36 gm
Carbohydrate:	15 gm
Fat:	8 gm=26%

INDIAN CHICKEN

2/3 cup	long grain rice
5 cloves	garlic
1	cinnamon stick
1	bay leaf
1 small	yellow onion, chopped
1 Tbsp	fresh ginger, minced, or
1/2 tsp	ground ginger
1 Tbsp	lemon juice
1/2 tsp	ground cumin
1/2 tsp	coriander
1/2 tsp	turmeric
1/4 tsp	ground cinnamon
1/8 tsp	cardamom
1/8 tsp	black pepper
1 cup	plain low fat yogurt
3 cups	white chicken or turkey meat, cubed and cooked
2 cups	red cabbage, shredded
1 small	tart green apple, cored and cubed, unpeeled

1. Preheat the oven to 350°. Cook the rice according to package directions, omitting the salt but adding 2 of the garlic cloves, cinnamon stick, and bay leaf. When the rice is done, discard the garlic, cinnamon, and bay leaf.

2. Meanwhile, in a blender or food processor, make a paste of the onion, ginger, lemon juice, cumin, coriander, turmeric, cinnamon, cloves, cardamom, pepper, and remaining garlic by blending for 10-15 seconds.

3. Transfer the paste to a large bowl and blend in the yogurt. Add the chicken, tossing to coat well.
4. Place the rice into an ungreased shallow 1 1/2-quart casserole, spoon the chicken mixture on top, cover, and bake for 35 minutes. Toward the end of the baking period, steam the red cabbage for 10 minutes over boiling water until it is tender but still crisp.
5. Cluster the red cabbage and apple in the center of the chicken mixture in a casserole dish.

Tip:

If you don't have exotic spices, omit them entirely and substitute 1 1/2 tsp curry powder.

Serves 4

Calories per serving:	370
Protein:	39 gm
Carbohydrate:	40 gm
Fat:	5 gm=12%

CHICKEN AND RICE CASSEROLE

	non-stick cooking spray
1	chicken, 2 1/2-3 lbs, cut into serving pieces and skinned
1/4 tsp	black pepper
1 1/2 tsp	olive oil
1 med	yellow onion, chopped fine
2 cloves	garlic, minced
1/2 cup	long grain rice
1/3 cup	dry white wine
3/4 cup	low sodium chicken broth
1 tsp	lemon rind, grated
1	bay leaf
1/2 tsp	dried thyme
1/2 tsp	rosemary, crumbled
1	9 oz pkg frozen artichoke hearts, cooked and drained
1 Tbsp	parsley, minced

1. Preheat the oven to 350°. Sprinkle the chicken with the pepper. Lightly coat a 4-quart Dutch oven with cooking spray, add the olive oil, and set over moderate heat for 30 seconds. Add the chicken and cook, turning occasionally, until no longer pink on the outside—about 5 minutes. Transfer to a platter and set aside.

2. Add the onion to the casserole and cook, uncovered, until soft—about 5 minutes; stir in the garlic and rice, and cook, stirring, for 1 minute. Add the wine, chicken broth, lemon rind, bay leaf, thyme, and rosemary, and bring to a simmer.

choke hearts, distributing them evenly. Cover with a piece of waxed paper, then the lid. Bake for 45-50 minutes or until the chicken is fork-tender and the rice fluffy. Discard the bay leaf and sprinkle with the parsley.

Serves 4

Calories per serving:	341
Protein:	33 gm
Carbohydrate:	28 gm
Fat:	11 gm=29%

GERMAN CHICKEN WITH CABBAGE AND APPLES

2–1 lb	whole chicken breasts, halved and skinned
1/2 tsp	black pepper
2 Tbsp	unsalted margarine
2	firm cooking apples, unpeeled, cored and cubed
1–1 lb	cabbage, cut into thick slices
2 med	carrots, peeled, quartered lengthwise, then cut into 2-inch lengths
1 med	yellow onion, sliced
1/4 cup	unsweetened apple juice
1 Tbsp	light brown sugar
1 1/2 tsp	cider vinegar
1/4 tsp	caraway seeds

1. Sprinkle the chicken breasts with the pepper. In a heavy 12-inch skillet, melt 1 Tbsp of the margarine over moderately high heat. Add the breasts and cook for 2 1/2 minutes on each side; transfer to a platter.
2. Reduce the heat to moderate, add the apples and cook, stirring frequently, until golden—about 5 minutes. Transfer to the platter with the chicken.
3. Melt the remaining margarine in the skillet and add the cabbage, carrots, and onion; cook, stirring, until tender but crisp—about 5 minutes. Stir in the apple juice, brown sugar, vinegar, and caraway seeds.
4. Return the chicken and half of the apples to the skillet. Reduce the heat to low; cover and simmer for 20 minutes. Transfer the chicken to a warm platter, ladle the

sauce over it, and garnish with the reserved apples.

Serves 4

Calories per serving:	310
Protein:	35 gm
Carbohydrate:	24 gm
Fat:	8 gm=25%

FRIED CHICKEN

2 oz	cornflakes, crushed
1 tsp	dry mustard
1/8 tsp	pepper
1/4 tsp	paprika
1/2 tsp	garlic powder
1	egg white
2 tsp	lemon juice
3 lbs	raw chicken breasts or legs

1. Preheat oven to 350°. Combine cornflakes, mustard, pepper, paprika, and garlic powder.
2. In a shallow bowl, combine egg white and lemon juice; beat slightly.
3. Dip chicken in egg mixture; coat with crumb mixture. Place into ungreased baking pan. Do not cover. Bake for 60 minutes.

Serves 4

Calories per serving:	340
Protein:	60 gm
Carbohydrate:	11 gm
Fat:	6 gm=16%

BAKED CHICKEN PARMESAN

6–5 oz	chicken fillets, skinned
2 oz	cornflakes, crushed
1/4 cup	grated Parmesan cheese
2 Tbsp	dried parsley, chopped
1/2 tsp	poultry seasoning
1/4 tsp	onion powder
1/8 tsp	garlic powder

1. Combine all ingredients except chicken and mix together in a small bowl. Place chicken, meaty side down, into baking pan.
2. Sprinkle 1 Tbsp of the mixture on each serving of chicken. Turn the chicken over and repeat. Sprinkle with paprika, if desired.
3. Bake at 350° for 60 minutes or until tender.

Serves 6

Calories per serving:	240
Protein:	38 gm
Carbohydrate:	10 gm
Fat:	5 gm=19%

BARBECUE CHICKEN KABOBS

1/2 cup	barbecue sauce
1/2 cup	water
1 clove	garlic, minced
2	chicken breasts, skinned, split, boned, and cut into 1-inch cubes
6 large	green onions, bias-sliced into 1-inch lengths
6 large	mushrooms, whole
4	cherry tomatoes

1. Combine barbecue sauce, water, garlic. Boil 1 minute and cool. Marinate chicken and green onions in mixture 30 minutes at room temperature, stirring once to coat all pieces.
2. Drain; reserve marinade.
3. Alternate chicken, mushrooms, and onion pieces on 4 skewers. Broil kabobs 4 inches from heat 4-5 minutes.
4. Place a cherry tomato on the end of each skewer, then turn; broil kabobs 4-5 minutes longer, brushing occasionally with barbecue marinade. Serve immediately.

Serves 4

Calories per serving:	273
Protein:	46 gm
Carbohydrate:	8 gm
Fat:	4.7 gm=16%

CALIFORNIA CHICKEN PUFFS

3	chicken breasts, cooked and diced
2 cups	cracked wheat, cooked (2 cups water and 1 1/3 cups cracked wheat)
1/2 cup	onion, diced
1/3 cup	celery, diced
1 cup	mushrooms, sliced
4 Tbsp	parsley, minced
1/8 tsp	black pepper
1 tsp	hot red pepper taco sauce
1/2 tsp	poultry seasoning
1/2 tsp	ground sage

1. Mix chicken and cracked wheat.
2. Sauté onion, celery, and mushrooms.
3. Add parsley, black pepper, taco sauce, poultry seasoning, and sage.
4. Form into 21 balls about 1 1/2 inches in diameter and place on non-stick baking sheet.
5. Bake at 350° for about 15 minutes. Serve plain, with undiluted cream of mushroom soup, or with your favorite sauce.

Serves 7

Calories per serving:	209
Protein:	19 gm
Carbohydrate:	27 gm
Fat:	1.5 gm=6%

CHICKEN AND BROCCOLI SKILLET

4 med	chicken breasts, boneless and skinless, cut into 1/2-inch strips
1/4 cup	onion, chopped
1 Tbsp	diet margarine
1	10 oz pkg broccoli, cut
1 tsp	lemon juice
1/4 tsp	thyme
3 med	tomatoes, cut into wedges

1. In a heavy 12-inch skillet, place the chicken, onion, and margarine. Cook until tender.
2. Stir in the broccoli, lemon juice, and thyme. Cover and cook for 6 minutes.
3. Add the tomatoes. Cook 3-4 minutes.

Serves 4

Calories per serving:	191
Protein:	30 gm
Carbohydrate:	8 gm
Fat:	4 gm=19%

CHICKEN A LA MEXICO

1/4 cup	orange juice
1 Tbsp	lime juice
2 tsp	cider vinegar
1 Tbsp	olive oil
1/2 tsp	oregano
1/2 tsp	salt
1/4 tsp	black pepper
2	chicken breasts, skinned, boned, and quartered

1. Prepare marinade by combining orange juice, lime juice, vinegar, olive oil, and seasonings. Pour over chicken and marinate in the refrigerator at least 2 hours. Drain, reserving marinade.
2. Prepare coals and cover the grill with aluminum foil.
3. Grill chicken over hot coals 10-12 minutes on each side or until chicken is cooked. Baste frequently with reserved marinade during cooking.

Serves 4

Calories per serving:	171
Protein:	27 gm
Carbohydrate:	2 gm
Fat:	5 gm=27%

SIMPLE STIR-FRY

1 lb	chicken breasts, skinned and boned
1 Tbsp	sake
2 Tbsp	potato starch
2 tsp	olive oil

1. Cut chicken breasts into cubes or strips. Toss with sake. Sprinkle with potato starch.
2. In a non-stick skillet, heat olive oil over medium-high heat. Add chicken and stir-fry 8-10 minutes or until done.

Serves 4

Calories per serving:	226
Protein:	35 gm
Carbohydrate:	3 gm
Fat:	7 gm=28%

TEXAS GRILLED CHICKEN

1/3 cup	lime juice, fresh squeezed
2 whole	chicken breasts, skinned, boned, and halved
1 cup	commercial or homemade tomato salsa

1. In a medium bowl, pour lime juice over chicken and marinate at room temperature 1 hour, turning to coat. Drain off marinade.
2. Prepare coals and cover the grill with aluminum foil. Grill chicken over hot coals 10-12 minutes on each side or until done. Place chicken on serving plates and drizzle salsa over top.

Serves 4

Calories per serving:	167
Protein:	27 gm
Carbohydrate:	6 gm
Fat:	5 gm=27%

CHICKEN ENCHILADAS

2	chicken breasts, skinned, boned
3 stalks	celery, cut into chunks
1 med	onion, cut into chunks
2 cloves	garlic
1 1/2 cups	chicken broth
8	flour or corn tortillas
2 oz	part-skim mozzarella cheese, thinly sliced
1/2 cup	enchilada sauce
1/2 cup	salsa

FILLING

1/2 med	green pepper, diced
1/2 med	white onion, diced
1 large	tomato, diced
1	3 1/2 oz can whole green chilies, diced
1/4 cup	chicken broth
1/4 tsp	salt
1/4 tsp	black pepper

1. In a medium pot, combine chicken, celery, onion chunks, garlic, and chicken broth, and bring to a boil. Cover, reduce heat, and simmer 30 minutes. Remove from heat. Let sit in broth 15 minutes.
2. Remove celery, onion, and garlic from broth and discard. Reserve remaining broth for later use. Tear chicken into strips.

To Prepare Filling:

1. In a medium pot, combine green pepper, diced onion, tomato, green chilies, chicken broth, salt, and pepper.
2. Cook over low heat 20 minutes or until vegetables are soft. Add chicken.

To Assemble:

1. Place 1/4 cup filling into each tortilla, along with a thin slice of mozzarella cheese and 1 tsp enchilada sauce.
2. Roll and place seam side down into a lightly greased 9x13-inch ovenproof baking dish.
3. Pour remaining enchilada sauce over top. Cover with aluminum foil. Bake at 350° 20-25 minutes or until hot. Accompany with tomato salsa.

Serves 8

Calories per serving:	220
Protein:	19 gm
Carbohydrate:	24 gm
Fat:	5 gm=21%

POLYNESIAN CHICKEN

1	6 oz can pineapple juice
2 Tbsp	lime juice
1 Tbsp	distilled white vinegar
6 cloves	garlic
1/2 tsp	salt
1/2 tsp	oregano
1/4 tsp	chili powder
1/4 tsp	black pepper
1 Tbsp	olive oil or canola oil
3	chicken breasts, skinned, boned, and halved

1. Prepare marinade by combining pineapple juice, lime juice, vinegar, garlic, salt, oregano, chili powder, pepper, and olive oil. Pour over chicken and marinate in the refrigerator 2 hours or as long as overnight.
2. Prepare coals and cover the grill with aluminum foil.
3. Drain off marinade and reserve.
4. Grill chicken over hot coals 6-8 minutes. Turn, baste with reserved marinade, and grill 6-8 minutes more. Turn and grill 5-10 minutes longer, turning frequently until chicken is cooked.

Serves 4

Calories per serving:	207
Protein:	27 gm
Carbohydrate:	9 gm
Fat:	7 gm=30%

CHICKEN BEAN BURRITOS

4	8 oz flour tortillas
2	chicken breasts, prepared as for Chicken a la Mexico
1/2 head	lettuce, shredded
1/2 cup	black bean dip
1/2 cup	salsa

1. Place tortillas between 2 slightly dampened paper towels. Microwave on high 1-2 minutes or until warm; keep wrapped until ready to serve.
2. To warm tortillas on stovetop, place them in a bamboo basket or vegetable steamer rack; steam in a covered pan over boiling water 3-5 minutes or until warm.
3. Slice chicken breasts into thin strips. Arrange lettuce, chicken, and bean dip on serving platter. Accompany with salsa and warm tortillas.

To Prepare Burrito:
1. Spoon bean dip along center of each warm tortilla. Divide chicken among tortillas and top with lettuce.
2. Fold opposite sides of each tortilla over filling. Fold ends over folded sides.

Serves 4

Calories per serving:	338
Protein:	3 gm
Carbohydrate:	31 gm
Fat:	9 gm=24%

215

CHICKEN CASSEROLE

2 med	chicken breasts, skinned, boned, and quartered
2 tsp	powdered rosemary
2 Tbsp	dried parsley
1/2 tsp	black pepper
1 whole	head garlic, separated into cloves and peeled
12	baby carrots
1 large	onion, cut into rings
4 small	red potatoes, halved
1 lb	fresh green beans
1 cup	dry white wine

1. In a covered casserole dish, arrange chicken on bottom.
2. Combine rosemary, parsley, and pepper. Sprinkle 1/3 of mixture over chicken.
3. Top with garlic, carrots, onion, and potatoes. Sprinkle 1/3 of seasoning mixture over potatoes.
4. Top with green beans. Sprinkle remaining 1/3 of seasoning over top. Pour wine over all.
5. Cover tightly with aluminum foil, then cover with lid. Bake at 350° 1 hour or until chicken is cooked and vegetables are tender.

Serves 6

Calories per serving:	242
Protein:	22 gm
Carbohydrate:	28 gm
Fat:	3 gm=11%

ORIENTAL CHICKEN

2	chicken breasts, skinned and cubed
1/4 cup	reduced-sodium soy sauce
1/2 cup	sake
1 tsp	granulated sugar
2 tsp	sesame oil
1	red onion, cut into cubes
	pepper
1/4 lb	fresh mushroom buttons
8	cherry tomatoes
1	zucchini, peeled and cubed
	olive oil for grill

1. Arrange chicken in a shallow dish.
2. In a bowl, combine soy sauce, sake, sugar, and sesame oil. Pour marinade over chicken and marinate 30 minutes at room temperature. Drain off marinade.
3. On skewers, alternate chicken, onion, pepper, mushrooms, tomatoes, and zucchini.
4. Prepare coals and brush the grill lightly with olive oil.
5. Grill kabobs 4-6 inches from heat, turning frequently and basting often, about 20 minutes or until chicken is done.

Serves 4

Calories per serving:	242
Protein:	30 gm
Carbohydrate:	11 gm
Fat:	7 gm=28%

KUNG PAO CHICKEN

1/2 cup	chicken broth	2 Tbsp	potato starch
1/3 cup	soy sauce	1 Tbsp	olive oil
1/2 cup	sake	2 large	clove garlic
1 clove	garlic, minced	1/2 lb	snow peas
1 tsp	hot chili oil	1	8 oz pkg water chestnuts
6	green onions, cut diagonally	2	dried negro chilies or other hot red chilies, reconstituted in water
2	chicken breasts, skinned, boned, and cut into strips 1/4-inch thick		

1. In a 2-quart saucepan, combine chicken broth, soy sauce, sake, minced garlic, and hot chili oil; let simmer while preparing the chicken.
2. Sprinkle chicken with 1 Tbsp of the potato starch. In a non-stick skillet, heat 2 tsp of the olive oil. Add chilies and garlic, and sauté 2-3 minutes. Add chicken and sauté about 10 minutes or until chicken is cooked. Remove chicken to a serving casserole.
3. Bring sauce to a boil. Dissolve remaining potato starch in 2 Tbsp cold water and gradually add to boiling broth. Cook and stir 2-3 minutes or until sauce thickens.
4. In the same non-stick skillet, heat remaining 1 tsp of olive oil. Add snow peas and water chestnuts, and stir-fry until snow peas are crisp-tender, about 2-3 minutes. Add green onions. Combine with chicken. Pour sauce over and toss.

Serves 4

Calories per serving:	343
Protein:	29 gm
Carbohydrate:	24 gm
Fat:	9 gm=23%

GARLIC CHICKEN

6 large	cloves garlic
3 Tbsp	olive oil
1 tsp	powdered rosemary
2 med	chicken breasts, skinned and boned
1 Tbsp	grated orange peel

1. In a blender or food processor, purée garlic with olive oil. Add rosemary and whirl 20 seconds. Arrange chicken breasts in an 8x8-inch baking dish. Sprinkle with orange peel. Pour marinade over all and marinate in the refrigerator 3-4 hours.
2. Drain off marinade. Bake chicken, uncovered, at 350° 30-35 minutes or until chicken is cooked.

Serves 4

Calories per serving:	194
Protein:	27 gm
Carbohydrate:	2 gm
Fat:	8 gm=37%

CHICKEN PARMESAN

1 tsp	paprika
3/4 tsp	white pepper
1/2 tsp	powdered rosemary
2	chicken breasts, skinned and boned
1/3 cup	vermouth
2 Tbsp	fresh lemon juice
1 cup	chicken broth
1/4 tsp	salt
1/4 tsp	arrowroot
1 Tbsp	cold water
1	14-oz can water packed artichokes, drained
1	8-oz can mushrooms, drained
1/4 cup	Parmesan cheese, freshly grated

1. Combine paprika, 1/2 tsp of the white pepper, and rosemary. Dredge chicken in seasoning to coat. Arrange chicken in a single layer in an 8x8-inch baking dish. Bake at 375° for 30 minutes or until chicken is cooked.
2. Meanwhile, in a 2-quart saucepan, combine vermouth, lemon juice, chicken broth, salt, and remaining 1/4 tsp white pepper, and bring to a boil. Reduce heat and simmer. When chicken is nearly cooked, bring mixture back to boiling, cook, stirring constantly, 2-3 minutes or until mixture thickens. Add artichokes and mushrooms.
3. Add tomatoes to chicken. Pour sauce over chicken and tomatoes. Sprinkle with cheese. Place under broiler 2-3 minutes or until cheese melts.

Serves 4

Calories per serving:	285
Protein:	35 gm
Carbohydrate:	20 gm
Fat:	6 gm=18%

LEMON AND HERB CHICKEN

12 oz	boneless, skinless chicken breasts
1	lemon, for juice
1/2 tsp	oregano
1	clove garlic
1/2 tsp	pepper, freshly ground
1/2 tsp	basil

1. Prepare breasts by pounding out between waxed paper. Squeeze lemon on breasts and add the herbs. Fold over.
2. Place breasts into a shallow dish and top with more lemon juice and herbs. Bake at 350° for 10-15 minutes. When done, slice breasts into medallions to serve.

Serves 2

Calories per serving:	138
Protein:	29 gm
Carbohydrate:	1 gm
Fat:	2 gm=13%

Chapter 20

Seafood
For Healthy Living

ORIENTAL TUNA

1/2 cup	green onions, sliced
1	8 oz can bamboo shoots, drained
1 cup	mushrooms, sliced
1 cup	peas
1/2 cup	water
1/4 tsp	bouillon granules
2 tsp	cornstarch
1/8 tsp	garlic powder
1/4 tsp	celery seeds
2	6 1/2 oz cans water-packed tuna
1	tomato, cut into wedges
2 1/2 cups	brown rice, cooked
5 tsp	soy sauce (optional)

1. Sauté onions, bamboo shoots, and mushrooms until crisp-tender. Add peas.
2. Combine water, bouillon granules, cornstarch, garlic powder, and celery seeds. Add to vegetables. Simmer 3 minutes or until thickened.
3. Stir in tuna and tomato. Heat thoroughly. Serve over 1/2 cup hot rice. Season with 1 tsp soy sauce.

Serves 5

Calories per serving:	276
Protein:	28 gm
Carbohydrate:	36 gm
Fat:	1 gm=4%

CREOLE

1/2 cup	onion, chopped
1/2 cup	green pepper, chopped
1 clove	garlic, minced
	cornstarch
1 tsp	chili powder
2 cups	tomatoes, chopped
2 Tbsp	parsley, snipped
1 lb	fish fillets or cleaned shrimp
3 cups	brown rice, cooked

1. Sauté onion, green pepper, and garlic until tender.
2. Whisk in cornstarch and chili powder.
3. Add tomatoes and parsley. Cook until thickened, stirring constantly. Simmer for 2 minutes.
4. Add shrimp or fish which has been cut into 1-inch cubes. Heat thoroughly.
5. Serve over 1/2 cup hot rice.

Serves 6

Calories per serving:	225
Protein:	16 gm
Carbohydrate:	31 gm
Fat:	1.5 gm=6%

HALIBUT STIR-FRY

	non-stick cooking spray
1 lb	cubed, halibut fillets
1 Tbsp	lemon juice
1 Tbsp	margarine
1 cup	carrots, thinly sliced
1 cup	celery, thinly sliced
1 bunch	green onions, chopped
1 cup	broccoli, chopped
1/4 tsp	ginger root, grated
1/4 cup	chicken broth
2 tsp	cornstarch
To taste	soy sauce and black pepper

1. In large skillet sprayed with cooking spray, lightly brown halibut and lemon juice. Place the steaks on a heated platter.
2. Melt the margarine in the skillet and sauté the carrots, celery, onions, broccoli, and ginger. Cook until vegetables are done but still crisp.
3. Return the steaks to the skillet.
4. In small bowl, combine the chicken broth and cornstarch. Pour the liquid into the skillet. Stir until thickened and the halibut flakes easily.
5. Season with soy sauce and pepper.

Serves 4

Calories per serving:	197
Protein:	29.4 gm
Carbohydrate:	10.3 gm
Fat:	4.6 gm=21%

FLORIDA FILLETS

2 lbs	fish fillets
1 Tbsp	diet margarine, melted
2 Tbsp	fresh orange juice
2 tsp	orange rind, grated
1 tsp	salt
Dash	pepper
Dash	nutmeg

1. Preheat the oven to 350°. Spray a baking dish with cooking spray. Place the fish fillets (skin side down) on the bottom of the dish.
2. In a medium-size bowl, combine the margarine, orange juice, orange rind, salt, pepper, and nutmeg. Pour over the fish.
3. Bake for 25-30 minutes or until the fish flakes easily with a fork. Serve on a bed of sliced orange rings.

Serves 6

Calories per serving:	184
Protein:	38 gm
Carbohydrate:	1 gm
Fat:	2 gm=10%

BAKED ORANGE ROUGHY

1 lb	orange roughy fillet
1 tsp	onion powder
1/4 cup	orange juice
2 Tbsp	lemon juice
2 Tbsp	dry white wine
1 tsp	fresh dill
1 Tbsp	cornstarch (mix with water to make paste)

1. Preheat the oven to 450°. Place roughy into a shallow baking dish.
2. In a small bowl, combine the onion powder, orange juice, lemon juice, wine, fresh dill, and cornstarch paste. Pour over the fish fillets. Cover dish tightly with aluminum foil.
3. Bake for 20 minutes.

Serves 3

Calories per serving:	141
Protein:	21 gm
Carbohydrate:	6 gm
Fat:	3 gm=19%

CRAB AND SHRIMP CASSEROLE

1 tsp	lemon juice
1 cup	low fat yogurt
2	6 1/2-oz cans crab, drained
1	4 1/2-oz can shrimp, drained
1	10-oz pkg frozen peas, thawed
1 1/2 cups	brown rice, cooked
1/4 cup	green pepper, chopped
2 Tbsp	parsley flakes

1. Whisk lemon juice into yogurt.
2. Add remaining ingredients and toss lightly.
3. Bake at 350° for 60 minutes in a covered 2-quart non-stick casserole dish.

Serves 6

Calories per serving:	191
Protein:	20 gm
Carbohydrate:	21 gm
Fat:	2.5 gm=12%

SHRIMP STIR-FRY

	non-stick cooking spray
1 1/2 cups	celery, sliced
1 clove	garlic
1 cup	onion, thinly sliced
1 Tbsp	water
1/2 tsp	fresh ginger, grated
10 oz	frozen peas, thawed
1 1/2 cups	mushrooms, sliced
1/3 cup	water
1 Tbsp	dry sherry
2 to 3 tsp	lemon juice
2 tsp	cornstarch
2 1/2 cups	shrimp, cleaned

1. Spray a heavy 10-inch skillet with cooking spray. Add the celery, garlic, onion, and water. Cook and stir for 2 minutes.
2. Add the ginger, peas, and mushrooms. Cook and stir 1 minute.
3. In a small bowl, combine the water, soy sauce, sherry, lemon juice, and cornstarch. Add to the vegetable mixture.
4. Fold in the shrimp. Cook and stir until sauce boils and thickens. Serve over rice.

Serves 6

Calories per serving:	154
Protein:	23 gm
Carbohydrate:	12 gm
Fat:	2 gm=12%

DILLED SALMON

1	8-oz bottle clam juice
1/2 cup	dry vermouth
1/2 cup	uncooked rice
2 Tbsp	lime juice
1 clove	garlic, crushed
2 tsp	dill, fresh
2	salmon steaks
1/2 cup	peas
1/4 cup	plain low fat yogurt

1. In a large skillet, combine the clam juice and dry vermouth. Bring to a boil.
2. Add the rice, lime juice, garlic, and dill. Mix well.
3. Add salmon steaks, cover, and simmer for 20 minutes.
4. Add the peas and cook for 2-3 minutes.
5. Place steaks over the rice on a serving dish and top with yogurt.

Serves 2

Calories per serving:	593
Protein:	38 gm
Carbohydrate:	51 gm
Fat:	10 gm=15%

TERIYAKI FISH

1 lb	fish (sword, tuna, or white)
1 Tbsp	apple juice
1/4 cup	teriyaki sauce
1 tsp	water

1. Mix the apple juice, teriyaki sauce, and water together.
2. Marinate the fish in sauce for 1 hour or more, turning occasionally.
3. Place on grill, in an aluminum foil pan. Baste with sauce. Cook on one side for 5 minutes; turn and cook for 5 more minutes until done.

Serves 4

Calories per serving:	118
Protein:	23 gm
Carbohydrate:	2 gm
Fat:	1 gm=8%

CAJUN FISH

	non-stick cooking spray
1/3 cup	onion, chopped
1/3 cup	green pepper, chopped
1 clove	garlic, minced
1/2 cup	water
1	16 oz can cut tomatoes
2 Tbsp	parsley flakes
1 Tbsp	instant chicken bouillon granules (low sodium)
Dash	red hot pepper sauce
1 Tbsp	cornstarch
3 Tbsp	water
1 lb	fish fillets, cut into 1-inch cubes

1. Spray a heavy 10-inch skillet with cooking spray. Place the onion, green pepper, garlic, and water in the skillet and cook, covered, until tender.
2. Add the tomatoes, parsley flakes, chicken bouillon, pepper sauce, and water to the skillet and simmer, covered, for 10 minutes.
3. Meanwhile, in small bowl, blend together the cornstarch and 3 Tbsp water. Stir into the tomato mixture. Cook and stir until thickened.
4. Add fish fillets. Simmer covered for 5-7 minutes. Serve over rice.

Serves 6

Calories per serving:	126
Protein:	19 gm
Carbohydrate:	5 gm
Fat:	3 gm=21%

SIMPLE SOLE

	non-stick cooking spray
1 med	onion, chopped
1/2 tsp	curry powder
1 large	tomato, chopped
3 oz	vegetable juice (low sodium)
Dash	salt
Dash	pepper
1 large	apple, thinly sliced
2 lbs	sole, cut into 1-inch slivers
1 Tbsp	parsley flakes

1. In skillet sprayed with cooking spray, sauté the onion until transparent. Add the curry powder, tomato, vegetable juice, salt, and pepper. Bring to a boil. Lower heat to medium and simmer for 5 minutes.
2. Add the apple, sole, and parsley flakes. Cook over low heat for 15-20 minutes or until fish is tender. Serve over rice.

Serves 6

Calories per serving:	162
Protein:	31 gm
Carbohydrate:	6 gm
Fat:	2 gm=11%

FILLET OF SOLE

2 lbs	fillets
	tarragon dressing
4 Tbsp	lemon juice
2 Tbsp	margarine
1 Tbsp	fresh tarragon leaves
1 Tbsp	chives
1/4 tsp	salt

1. Preheat the oven to 350°. Brush the sole lightly with tarragon dressing. Sprinkle with 2 Tbsp of lemon juice. Place into a 13x9-inch baking dish sprayed with cooking spray. Cover with aluminum foil and bake for 20 minutes.
2. Meanwhile in small saucepan, combine the margarine, tarragon leaves, chives, and salt. Heat slightly. Add the remaining 2 Tbsp of lemon juice.
3. To serve, place the fillets on a platter; pour the sauce over them.

Serves 6

Calories per serving:	173
Protein:	31 gm
Carbohydrate:	2 gm
Fat:	5 gm=26%

BAKED CRAB

1	egg white
1/4 cup	honey mustard
1/8 tsp	dry mustard
2 tsp	steak sauce
1 Tbsp	lemon juice
2	7 1/2-oz cans king crab meat
2 Tbsp	green pepper, chopped
2	slices wheat bread, cubed
1/4 cup	fat-free cheddar cheese

1. In a small bowl, combine first 5 ingredients.
2. In a large bowl, toss lightly crab, green pepper, and bread.
3. Pour sauce over mixture and toss. Turn into 1-quart baking dish. Bake at 400° for 10 minutes. Sprinkle on cheese and continue to bake for 5 more minutes or until cheese is melted.

Serves 4

Calories per serving:	194
Protein:	25 gm
Carbohydrate:	12 gm
Fat:	5.5 gm=26%

RED SNAPPER IN A SNAP

1 cup	onion, chopped
1/2 cup	green onion, chopped
2 cups	tomato, chopped
1/2 cup	red wine
2 cloves	garlic, minced
1/4 tsp	thyme, diced
1/4 tsp	marjoram, diced
1/4 tsp	allspice
1/4 tsp	black pepper, freshly ground
1	bay leaf
Pinch	cayenne
1 lb	red snapper fillets

1. Heat a skillet large enough to hold the fish. Dry cook onion and green onion, stirring, until they color.
2. Add all remaining ingredients except the fish. Cover the skillet and simmer for 2 minutes.
3. Lay the fish in the sauce, cover the skillet, and simmer for 8 minutes. Carefully turn fish. Cover and simmer for 10 minutes more, until the fish flakes apart at the touch of a fork.

Serves 2

Calories per serving:	298
Protein:	47.9 gm
Carbohydrate:	19.6 gm
Fat:	3.6 gm=11%

CATFISH CAKES

1	6 oz catfish fillet, chopped
2	slices stale bread, crushed
1/4 cup	water
1 Tbsp	green onion, minced
1 tsp	fresh parsley, minced
1	egg white
1 tsp	fresh lemon juice
1/2 tsp	powdered mustard
1/8 tsp	black pepper, freshly ground
1	egg white
1/4 cup	skim milk
1/4 cup	bread crumbs
1	lemon, quartered

1. Preheat the oven to 375°. Combine the first 9 ingredients and make 4 cakes, using your hands to pat them into patties as you would hamburgers.
2. Whisk the egg white with the skim milk; dip the patties into the mixture, then coat them with the bread crumb mix.
3. Bake on lightly greased or non-stick baking sheet for 12 minutes.

Serves 2

Calories per serving:	194
Protein:	22.7 gm
Carbohydrate:	17.2 gm
Fat:	4.2 gm=20%

FILLET SO SIMPLE

	non-stick cooking spray
4	fish fillets (any white flaky fish)
4 tsp	lemon pepper
1	lime or lemon
8	spring onions
	parsley

1. Preheat dry skillet for 5 minutes on medium. A cast iron skillet works best. (Make sure to have the ventilation fan on, for this may smoke some.)
2. Spray both sides of the fillets with the spray and sprinkle 1 tsp of the lemon pepper on each fillet. Cook about 2 minutes per side for average size fillets.
3. For serving, chop spring onions and place a small pile on each fillet. Squeeze a slice of lime over all and garnish with parsley and lime slices.

Serves 4

Calories per serving:	102
Protein:	22 gm
Carbohydrate:	1 gm
Fat:	1 gm=9%

SHRIMP ÉTOUFFÉE

1 cup	onion, chopped
1/2 cup	green onion, chopped
1/2 cup	celery, chopped
1/4 cup	bell pepper, chopped
2 Tbsp	dry brown roux*
1/2 cup	water
3 cloves	garlic, minced
1/4 tsp	dried thyme
1/8 tsp	black pepper, freshly ground
Pinch	cayenne
6 oz	raw shrimp, peeled
1 1/2 cups	cooked rice

1. Cook the onion, green onion, celery, and bell pepper in a saucepan over high heat, stirring frequently until vegetables color slightly, about 2 minutes.
2. Add the roux and blend in the water. Add all seasonings and simmer slowly for 20 minutes.
3. Add shrimp and cook for 2 minutes, or just until they turn pink. Serve over brown rice.

*Dry Roux

The traditional roux is a mixture of half flour and half fat but making a roux without the oil is simple.

1 cup	all-purpose flour

1. Put the flour into a heavy skillet and place over moderate heat.

2. Stir the flour around often with a wooden spoon as it cooks.

3. Pay attention to the cooking because the flour will take a 5–7 minutes, to begin coloring. At this point you have roux. For the next 5–7 minutes it will darken until it reaches a light wood color. Stir constantly to keep the flour in the bottom of the skillet moving so it will not burn, and so all the flour in the pan will color evenly. The whole process takes about 15 minutes of close attention to get a nice, rich roux.

Serves 8

Calories per serving:	320
Protein:	21 gm
Carbohydrate:	55 gm
Fat:	1.7 gm=5%

FLOUNDER STUFFED
WITH CRAB

1/4 cup	chopped onion
1/4 cup	chopped green onion
2 Tbsp	chopped celery
1 Tbsp	green bell pepper, minced
1 clove	garlic, minced
1 tsp	fresh parsley, minced
1/8 tsp	dried thyme
1/4 cup	bread crumbs
To taste	black pepper, freshly ground
1/4 cup	water
1	egg white
2 oz	crab meat
2	3-oz flounder fillets, skin off
1/4 cup	dry white wine
Pinch	paprika
1 tsp	cornstarch
1 Tbsp	water
1/2 tsp	fresh lemon juice

1. Cook the onion, green onion, celery, bell pepper, garlic, parsley, and thyme over medium heat, stirring, until they begin to brown slightly. Blend in the bread crumbs. Remove from the heat and season with pepper.
2. Moisten the mixture with the water and blend in the egg white. Fold in the crab meat.
3. Preheat the oven to 350°. Divide the stuffing in half and shape into balls. Wrap a flounder fillet around each

ball and secure with a toothpick, or tie around with a string.

4. Set the fillet seam side up in a baking dish. Pour wine over and sprinkle with paprika. Cover dish and bake for 30 minutes.

5. Carefully transfer the fish to warm plates. Measure the cooking liquid, add enough water to it to make 1/2 cup, and return it to the pan. Blend the cornstarch with the Tbsp water and add it to the cooking liquid. Season with the lemon juice and pepper and stir over low heat just until hot. Spoon the sauce over the fish.

Serves 2

Calories per serving:	202
Protein:	25.8 gm
Carbohydrate:	14.2 gm
Fat:	2.4 gm=11%

LOUISIANA CREOLE

2/3 cup	onion, chopped
1/3 cup	green bell pepper, chopped
1 cup	tomato, chopped
1 clove	garlic, minced
1 tsp	parsley, chopped
1/2 tsp	paprika
1/4 tsp	dried thyme
Pinch	cayenne
To taste	black pepper, freshly ground
6 oz	raw shrimp, peeled
1 cup	hot cooked white rice,

1. Cook the onion and bell pepper in a saucepan over medium heat for 2 minutes, stirring frequently to keep from sticking. Add the tomato and all the herbs and seasonings.
2. Let the mixture come to a simmer and continue simmering for 2 minutes. Add the shrimp and simmer only long enough for them to become pink and just cooked, about 2 minutes.
3. Spoon 1/2 cup of the rice onto the center of each plate and ladle the creole around it in a circle.

Serves 2

Calories per serving:	233
Protein:	19.6 gm
Carbohydrate:	36.2 gm
Fat:	3.1 gm=12%

COLD CRAB

1	ripe tomato, finely chopped
3 Tbsp	olive oil
1/2 cup	fresh lemon juice
3/4 tsp	salt or to taste
1/2 tsp	black pepper
1 bunch	fresh parsley
2 lbs	crab, cooked and cleaned
1	lemon, cut into wedges

1. In a sauce dish or gravy boat, combine tomato, olive oil, lemon juice, salt, and pepper.
2. Line a platter with parsley and arrange crab on it. Garnish with lemon wedges. Pass the sauce.

Serves 4

Calories per serving:	115
Protein:	22 gm
Carbohydrate:	3 gm
Fat:	2 gm=16%

CALAMARI STIR-FRY

1 lb	squid tubes, cleaned and stripped
1 Tbsp	olive oil
1 Tbsp	ginger root, finely minced
3 cloves	garlic, minced
1 med	white onion, thinly sliced
1	red pepper, thinly sliced
1	green pepper, thinly sliced
1/3 lb	fresh mushrooms, thinly sliced
1	8-oz can sliced water chestnuts, drained
3 stalks	celery, thinly sliced
1/4 cup	bottled oyster sauce
1 Tbsp	reduced-sodium soy sauce
1/2 tsp	sesame oil

1. In a non-stick skillet, toss squid tubes with 1 tsp of the olive oil and sauté over medium heat 2-3 minutes or until squid turns white. Remove from heat.
2. In a wok, heat remaining olive oil. Add ginger root, garlic and onions, and stir-fry 3-4 minutes or until onions begin to soften. Add peppers, mushrooms, water chestnuts, and celery, and stir-fry 2-3 minutes or just until peppers are tender. Add squid. Combine oyster sauce, soy sauce, and sesame oil; pour over vegetables and squid.

Serves 4

Calories per serving:	220
Protein:	21 gm
Carbohydrate:	20 gm
Fat:	6 gm=25%

GARLIC MUSSELS AND CLAMS

1/4 cup	dry white wine
2 1/2 Tbsp	olive oil
8 large	cloves of garlic
	juice of 1 lemon
1/2 tsp	salt
1/4 tsp	black pepper
3 lb	clams, cleaned
1 lb	mussels, cleaned

1. In a small bowl, mix all ingredients except clams and mussels.
2. In large steamer over boiling water, combine all ingredients. Cover and steam 5-10 minutes, removing each clam and mussel as it opens.

Serves 4

Calories per serving:	207
Protein:	29 gm
Carbohydrate:	9 gm
Fat:	5 gm=22%

MUSSELS AND CLAMS ITALIANO

2 Tbsp	fresh basil
2 Tbsp	olive oil
1/4 cup	parsley, minced
1 Tbsp	garlic, minced
1/2 cup	dry white wine
1/2 tsp	salt
1/4 tsp	black pepper
1/2 tsp	crushed red pepper
4 large	ripe tomatoes, diced
3 lbs	mussels, cleaned
1 lb	clams, cleaned

1. In a small bowl, mix all ingredients except mussels and clams.
2. In a larger steamer over boiling water, combine all the ingredients. Cover and steam 5-10 minutes, removing each clam and mussel as it opens.

Serves 4

Calories per serving:	263
Protein:	29 gm
Carbohydrate:	15 gm
Fat:	8 gm=28%

SMOKED SALMON

3 cups	hickory chips
1 1/2 lbs	salmon steak
1 1/2 lbs	cod steak
2 tsp	olive oil
1	bunch cilantro or parsley
2	lemons, cut into wedges

1. Soak hickory chips in water about 1 hour. Drain thoroughly. Prepare coals and cover the grill with aluminum foil.
2. Rub fish with olive oil. When coals are ready, sprinkle hickory chips over the coals. (The hickory will smoke for about 15 minutes, so put the seafood on at once.) Cook seafood on grill 10 minutes per inch of thickness of fish. If grill has a lid, keep it down during cooking.
3. Line serving platter with cilantro or parsley. Arrange cod and salmon on top. Split each steak in half lengthwise and garnish with lemons.

Serves 4

Calories per serving:	153
Protein:	25 gm
Carbohydrate:	6 gm
Fat:	4 gm=24%

SEAFOOD MEDLEY

1 cup	chicken broth
1/2 cup	dry vermouth
1/4 cup	fresh lemon juice
1/4 tsp	salt
1/4 tsp	white pepper
1 lb	sole fillets
1 tsp	olive oil or canola oil
1 Tbsp	finely chopped leek, white part only
1/4 lb	fresh mushrooms, sliced
1 1/2 tsp	arrowroot
3 Tbsp	cold water
1/4 lb	shrimp meat, cooked
1/4 lb	crab meat, cooked
1/3 cup	Parmesan cheese, freshly grated

1. In skillet, combine chicken broth, vermouth, and lemon juice, and bring to a boil. Add salt and white pepper. Place sole into the liquid; cover and poach 4-5 minutes or until fish is barely cooked. Remove sole from stock and drain on paper towels. Transfer stock to a saucepan and bring to a boil. Reduce heat and simmer, uncovered, 5 minutes to reduce to 1 cup.
2. In the same skillet, heat olive oil. Add leek and mushrooms, and sauté 4-5 minutes or until mushrooms are tender.
3. Bring fish stock back to boiling. Dissolve arrowroot in cold water and gradually add to fish stock. Cook and stir until stock begins to thicken. Add shrimp, crab, and half the cheese. Arrange sole in ovenproof baking dish. Pour sauce over sole. Sprinkle with remaining

cheese. Broil 2-3 minutes or until cheese is melted.

Serves 4

Calories per serving:	261
Protein:	39 gm
Carbohydrate:	4 gm
Fat:	6 gm=21%

Chapter 21

Turkey
For Healthy Living

STUFFED TURKEY WITH YAMS

	non-stick cooking spray
3 large	sweet potatoes (about 2 lbs), peeled and cut into 2-inch pieces
1 large	orange, juiced and rind grated
2 Tbsp	unsalted margarine
1 large	yellow onion, chopped
1 med	carrot, peeled and chopped
1 med	stalk celery, chopped
1/2 cup	parsnip, peeled and chopped
1 tsp	dried sage, crumbled
1	fresh turkey breast (about 5 lbs)

1. Preheat the oven to 450°. Place the sweet potatoes into a medium-size saucepan, cover with boiling unsalted water, and cook, covered, for 15 minutes or until tender when pierced with a knife. Drain well and mash. Stir in the grated orange rind.

2. Meanwhile, melt 1 Tbsp of the margarine in a 10-inch skillet over moderate heat. Add the onion, carrot, celery, and parsnip, cook for 10 minutes, stirring frequently. Add the sage. Blend the mixture into the mashed sweet potatoes. Let the mixture cool slightly, then spoon into both cavities of the turkey breast. Secure the neck skin with toothpicks.

3. Lightly coat a 13x9x2-inch baking pan with the cooking spray. Place the turkey breast into the pan and rub the skin with the remaining margarine. Insert a meat thermometer into the thickest part and roast for 30 minutes. Reduce the oven temperature to 375° and roast, basting occasionally with the orange juice, for 45

more minutes or until the thermometer registers 180°. If the turkey browns too quickly, cover it loosely with aluminum foil.

4. Remove from the oven and let stand at room temperature for 10 minutes before carving.

Serves 10

Calories per serving:	323
Protein:	43 gm
Carbohydrate:	21 gm
Fat:	7 gm=20%

TURKEY SOUFFLÉ

	non-stick cooking spray
1 cup	skim milk
3 Tbsp	flour
1 small	yellow onion
2	whole cloves
1	bay leaf
1/4 tsp	ground sage
1/4 tsp	paprika
1/4 tsp	hot red pepper sauce
1/4 tsp	salt
1/8 tsp	ground nutmeg
2 large	eggs, separated
3 large	egg whites
3/4 cup	turkey, cooked and chopped
1/4 cup	carrots, cooked and chopped
1/4 cup	frozen tiny peas

1. Preheat the oven to 400°. In a medium-size heavy saucepan over low heat, whisk the milk into the flour. Stud the onion with the cloves and add to the pan along with the bay leaf. Cook, stirring, until quite thick—about 5 minutes. Remove from the heat and discard the onion, cloves, and bay leaf. Stir in the sage, paprika, red pepper sauce, salt, and nutmeg; set aside.
2. In a large bowl, whisk the egg yolks until just blended. Quickly stir in a little of the hot milk mixture, then stir all back into the saucepan. Stir in the turkey, carrots, and peas.
3. Beat the 5 egg whites until stiff but not dry. Gently

fold into the turkey-vegetable mixture.

4. Lightly coat a 1 1/2-quart soufflé dish with the cooking spray. Pour in the turkey mixture and bake, uncovered, about 25 minutes or until puffy and golden. Serve immediately, before the soufflé has a chance to fall.

Serves 4

Calories per serving:	158
Protein:	17 gm
Carbohydrate:	11 gm
Fat:	5 gm=28%

BROWN RICE STUFFING

2 cups	brown rice, uncooked
6 cups	chicken stock
3	onions, chopped
4 stalks	celery, chopped
1	green pepper, chopped
3	egg whites, stiffly beaten
8 oz	mushrooms, chopped
1 Tbsp	parsley, dried
1 Tbsp	pimento, chopped

1. Cook rice in chicken stock until tender—about 40 minutes.
2. Sauté onion celery, and green pepper until tender.
3. Fold in stiffly beaten egg whites, mushrooms, parsley, and pimento.
4. Bake in a covered casserole dish at 350° for 1 hour, or use to stuff a turkey.

Serves 12

Calories per serving:	135
Protein:	4 gm
Carbohydrate:	30 gm
Fat:	Trace

JAMBALAYA

	non-stick cooking spray
1 lb	turkey cutlets, cut into 1/2-inch strips
2 stalks	celery, chopped
1	green pepper, chopped
1	onion, chopped
2	14 1/2 oz cans stewed tomatoes
1	13 3/4 oz can chicken broth
1	10 oz pkg cut okra, frozen
2	bay leaves
1 tsp	dried thyme
1/2 tsp	ground red pepper
2 cups	uncooked long grain rice

1. Coat large non-stick skillet with cooking spray. Heat skillet over medium-high heat. Sauté turkey cutlets in skillet 4 minutes or until cooked through. Remove turkey and place on a plate; keep warm.
2. In the same skillet, sauté celery, pepper, and onion 4 minutes or until tender. Add tomatoes, chicken broth, okra, bay leaves, thyme, and ground red pepper. Bring to boil; stir in rice; reduce heat and simmer, covered, for 5-18 minutes, until rice is tender.
3. Add turkey cutlets; cook 1 minute or until heated thoroughly. Remove bay leaves before serving.

Serves 6-8

Calories per serving:	380
Protein:	25 gm
Carbohydrate:	64 gm
Fat:	8 gm=19%

TORTILLAS

2	6-inch tortillas
1 tsp	olive oil
1/3 lb	turkey breast cutlet
1 tsp	lime juice
1/4 tsp	red hot pepper sauce
2	avocados, sliced (optional)
1/2 cup	iceberg lettuce, shredded
1 small	tomato, cored and chopped
2	yellow onions, sliced thin
2 Tbsp	plain low fat yogurt

1. Preheat the oven to 250°. Wrap the tortillas in aluminum foil and warm them about 5 minutes.
2. Meanwhile, in a heavy 10-inch skillet, heat the olive oil over high heat for 1 minute. Add the turkey cutlet and cook for 2-3 minutes on each side or until lightly browned. Transfer the turkey to a cutting board and slice across the grain into thin strips. In a medium-size bowl, toss the turkey strips with the lime juice and red pepper sauce.
3. Place equal amounts of the turkey, avocado, lettuce, tomato, and onion rings in the center of each warm tortilla. Top with the yogurt and fold the tortilla over the filling. Serve immediately.

Serves 2

Calories per serving:	236
Protein:	21 gm
Carbohydrate:	22 gm
Fat:	7 gm=27%

TURKEY ASPARAGUS

10 oz	frozen cut asparagus
3 cups	cooked turkey, cut into strips
1/2 cup	chicken stock
2 Tbsp	red wine vinegar or lemon juice
1 1/2 cup	brown rice, cooked
1 1/2 cup	wild rice, cooked
Garnish	almonds, slivered (optional)

1. Cook asparagus and drain.
2. Add asparagus, turkey, chicken stock, and vinegar or lemon juice to combined rices. Toss gently together.
3. Heat and season to taste.
4. Garnish with slivered almonds before serving.

Serves 8

Calories per serving:	189
Protein:	22 gm
Carbohydrate:	17 gm
Fat:	4 gm=19%

TURKEY FAJITAS

1/4 cup	fresh lime juice
1/4 cup	reduced sodium soy sauce
2 Tbsp	olive oil
2 whole	turkey breasts, sliced thinly
1 med	white onion, cut into thin wedges
1 med	green pepper, cut into thin strips
1 med	red pepper, cut into thin strips
1 large	tomato, cut into thin strips
4	8-inch flour tortillas, warmed
1/2 cup	salsa

1. Prepare marinade by combining lime juice, soy sauce, and olive oil. Pour 2/3 of the marinade over turkey and marinate in the refrigerator 1-2 hours, turning once or twice.
2. Remove turkey from marinade with a slotted spoon; grill or pan-fry turkey 4-5 minutes per side.
3. Meanwhile, in a wok or heavy skillet, heat remaining 1/3 marinade. Stir-fry onion and peppers 2-3 minutes. Toss with turkey and tomato. Garnish with salsa. Serve with warm tortillas.

Serves 4

Calories per serving:	366
Protein:	32 gm
Carbohydrate:	28 gm
Fat:	14 gm=34%

ROASTED TURKEY

1 tsp	garlic powder
1 tsp	dried thyme
1 tsp	dried basil
1 tsp	black pepper
1/2 tsp	white pepper
1/2 tsp	cayenne pepper
2 lbs	fresh turkey breast

1. Combine seasonings. Rub turkey with generous amount of seasoning.
2. Roast on a rack at 350° for 1 1/2 hours or until done.

Serves 8

Calories per serving:	139
Protein:	30 gm
Carbohydrate:	Trace
Fat:	1 gm=6%

LOUISIANA TURKEY

1	egg
1/3 cup	brown sugar
1/3 cup	cider vinegar
1/3 cup	dry mustard
1/4 tsp	salt
1 Tbsp	oregano
2 tsp	ground cumin
1 tsp	chili powder
1 tsp	dried thyme
1/2 tsp	cayenne
1 Tbsp	potato starch
2	turkey breasts, skinned, boned, and cut into strips
2 tsp	olive oil
4	8-inch tortillas
1/2 head	iceberg lettuce, shredded

1. In the top of a double boiler, beat egg. Add sugar and beat; then add vinegar and dry mustard, and beat. Place top of double boiler over boiling water and cook 5-10 minutes, stirring often or until sauce thickens. Season with salt. Set aside.

2. In a pie plate, combine oregano, cumin, chili powder, thyme, cayenne, and potato starch. Toss turkey strips in mixture until evenly coated.

3. In a non-stick skillet, heat olive oil. Add turkey strips and brown over high heat 4-5 minutes, stirring often. Reduce heat to low and continue cooking about 15 minutes or until turkey is cooked.

4. When turkey is nearly done, warm the tortillas. Fold

warm tortillas into fourths and tuck into a napkin-lined basket.

5. Line an oval serving platter with shredded lettuce. Arrange turkey strips over lettuce. Place a dollop of sauce at each end of platter. Serve at once. To eat, fill each tortilla with lettuce and turkey, and dip into sauce.

Serves 4

Calories per serving:	430
Protein:	35 gm
Carbohydrate:	46 gm
Fat:	12 gm=25%

ORIENTAL TURKEY

2 tsp	olive oil
1 large	onion, chopped
4 cloves	garlic, minced
1/4 cup	all-purpose flour
1 tsp	cayenne pepper
2	turkey breast fillets, quartered
1	16 oz can plum Italian tomatoes, chopped
2 3/4 cups	chicken broth
1/8 tsp	powdered saffron
1/2 tsp	salt or to taste
1 1/3 cups	long grain rice, uncooked
1 1/2 cups	cooked peas

1. In a skillet, heat olive oil. Add onion and garlic, and sauté 6-8 minutes or until onion is just tender.
2. Combine flour and cayenne. Dredge turkey in flour mixture. Add to skillet and brown 2-3 minutes on each side. Add tomatoes, chicken broth, saffron, and salt, and bring to a boil. Stir in rice. Cover and simmer 30-45 minutes or until rice is tender and turkey is cooked. Stir in peas. Serve at once.

Serves 6

Calories per serving:	352
Protein:	26 gm
Carbohydrate:	49 gm
Fat:	5 gm=13%

TURKEY PRIMAVERA

2	turkey breasts, skinned, halved
3/4 cup	dry white wine
1 cup	chicken broth
1 Tbsp	tomato paste
1 tsp	thyme
1 Tbsp	parsley, minced
1 large	white onion, sliced
3 large	cloves garlic, minced
1 Tbsp	olive oil
2	green peppers, sliced
1 pint	cherry tomatoes, halved

1. In a large non-stick skillet, brown turkey breasts 5-7 minutes on each side. In a saucepan, warm wine, chicken broth, tomato paste, parsley, and thyme; pour over browned turkey breasts. Reduce heat and simmer, uncovered, 20-30 minutes, basting with sauce and turning often.
2. In a medium non-stick skillet, sauté onion and garlic in olive oil 7-10 minutes or until onions are softened. Remove from heat; add green peppers and tomatoes. Just before serving, add to turkey; raise heat to high and cook 2-3 minutes or until sauce is bubbly and peppers and onions are warmed.

Serves 4

Calories per serving:	272
Protein:	30 gm
Carbohydrate:	14 gm
Fat:	7 gm=23%

ARTICHOKE TURKEY

1/4 tsp ea	black pepper and salt
1 tsp	powdered rosemary
1 tsp	paprika
2	turkey breasts, skinned
2 tsp	olive oil or canola oil
1	14-oz can water-packed artichoke hearts
1/4 lb	fresh mushrooms, sliced
2	green onions, chopped
2/3 cup	chicken broth
1/4 cup	dry sherry
2 Tbsp	all-purpose flour
2 Tbsp	water

1. In a shallow pan, combine seasonings and dredge turkey in mixture. In a non-stick skillet, heat oil. Add turkey and brown 3-5 minutes on each side.
2. Arrange turkey in a 2-quart baking dish. Tuck artichokes in between. To the skillet, add mushrooms and onions; sauté 2-3 minutes. Add chicken broth and sherry; bring to a boil. Combine flour with water. Add to broth mixture, stirring constantly 2-3 minutes. Pour sauce over turkey and artichokes. Cover with aluminum foil.
3. Bake at 375° for 40 minutes.

Serves 4

Calories per serving:	231
Protein:	29 gm
Carbohydrate:	10 gm
Fat:	6 gm=23%

TURKEY LOAF

1/3 cup	barley
2 cups	tomato sauce
1/4 cup	water
2 Tbsp	dry mustard
3 Tbsp	cider vinegar
3/4 lb	turkey breast, ground
1/3 cup	green onions, chopped
1	egg
4 cloves	garlic, finely minced
1/4 tsp	black pepper

1. In 1 cup of water, soak the barley overnight. Drain.
2. In a small bowl, combine 1 cup tomato sauce, water, mustard, and vinegar. Set aside. Combine barley, ground turkey, green onions, egg, garlic, pepper, and 1/2 cup of the sauce. Mix thoroughly. Arrange in a loaf pan. Pour an additional 1/2 cup sauce over top.
3. Bake at 325° for 1 hour. Serve with remaining sauce.

Serves 8

Calories per serving:	128
Protein:	16 gm
Carbohydrate:	13 gm
Fat:	2 gm=14%

HOT AND SPICY TURKEY

1	2 lb turkey breast
1 cup	hot chili sauce
1/2 cup	salsa

1. Roast turkey on a rack in a 350° oven for 1 1/2 hours; baste with 1/2 cup hot chili sauce. Cook 45 minutes more or until turkey is cooked, basting frequently.
2. In a small saucepan, combine remaining 1/2 cup chili sauce with salsa, and heat. Pass the sauce with turkey.

Serves 9

Calories per serving:	140
Protein:	27 gm
Carbohydrate:	4 gm
Fat:	1 gm=6%

Chapter 22

Desserts

For Healthy Living

APPLE RINGS

1 small	Granny Smith apple, cored and cut into 4 rings
1/2 cup	diet cherry soda
1/8 tsp	ground allspice
1/8 tsp	cinnamon

1. In small skillet, over medium-high heat, combine apples, soda, and spices.
2. Cook 5-7 minutes, turning apples once, until sauce is slightly thickened and apples are tender.

Serves 1

Calories per serving:	65
Protein:	0 gm
Carbohydrate:	17 gm
Fat:	0 gm

HOMEMADE
CHOCOLATE PUDDING

1 oz	unsweetened chocolate
2 cups	skim milk
1/3 cup	sugar
3 Tbsp	cornstarch
1 tsp	vanilla extract

1. In the bottom half of a medium-size double boiler, bring about 1 cup water to a simmer over moderate heat—about 2 minutes. Place the chocolate into the top half of the double boiler and melt it over the gently bubbling water in the bottom half—about 2 minutes. Stir in 1 3/4 cups of the milk and the sugar, cover, and heat for 3 minutes or until the milk is very hot.
2. In a measuring cup, blend the cornstarch with the remaining milk; stir into the hot chocolate mixture. Cook, stirring constantly, until the mixture has thickened and is smooth—about 1 minute. Cover and cook 15 minutes longer, then mix in the vanilla extract.
3. Spoon the pudding into serving bowls, cover with plastic wrap, and refrigerate at least 3 hours before serving.

Serves 4

Calories per serving:	168
Protein:	5 gm
Carbohydrate:	30 gm
Fat:	4 gm=21%

APPLE BREAD PUDDING

2 cups	skim milk
2 small	apples, cored and diced
4	1 oz slices day-old bread, cubed
1/4 cup	granulated light brown sugar
1/2 cup	walnuts, chopped
1/4 tsp	ground cardamom
2 large	eggs, lightly beaten
1/2 tsp	vanilla extract
1/4 tsp	ground nutmeg

1. In a 4-cup microwave-safe dish, microwave milk and apples on high 4 minutes, until hot but not boiling.
2. In a 6-cup microwave-safe soufflé dish, combine bread, sugar, walnuts, and cardamom; set aside.
3. In small bowl, combine eggs and vanilla; gradually whisk 1/2 cup hot milk into the egg mixture.
4. Stir egg mixture into remaining milk. Add nutmeg and milk mixture to soufflé dish; stir to combine.
5. Microwave on high, 2 minutes, stirring once; microwave on medium, 1 1/2 minutes; gently push outer edges toward center; microwave on medium 1 1/2 minutes longer, until almost set in middle.
6. Let stand 30 minutes; serve warm or cold.

Serves 4

Calories per serving:	252
Protein:	10 gm
Carbohydrate:	39 gm
Fat:	6 gm=21%

STRAWBERRY CREAM

2 cups	strawberries
1 cup	fat-free sour cream
4 Tbsp	skim milk
1 Tbsp	sugar

1. Whisk together sour cream, skim milk, and sugar. Let stand at room temperature for 30 minutes.
2. Slice berries and place in serving dish. Pour cream over all and serve.

Serves 2

Calories per serving:	90
Protein:	12 gm
Carbohydrate:	20 gm
Fat:	Trace

DATE PUMPKIN SPICE BARS

1 1/2 cups	all-purpose flour
2 tsp	baking powder
2 tsp	pumpkin pie spice
1/2 tsp	baking soda
1/2 cup	margarine, softened
1 cup	light brown sugar, firmly packed
2	eggs
1 cup	canned solid packed pumpkin
1 cup	bran
1 cup	dates, chopped
	powdered sugar (optional)

1. In small bowl, combine flour, baking powder, pumpkin pie spice, and baking soda. In large bowl, with electric mixer, beat margarine and brown sugar at medium speed until creamy. Beat in eggs and pumpkin.
2. Stir in flour mixture, bran, and dates. Spread batter into 2 greased 8-inch square baking pans.
3. Bake at 350° for 30 minutes or until toothpick inserted comes out clean. Remove from pans; cool on wire racks. Dust with powdered sugar if desired; cut each panful into 12 bars.

PAN VARIATION:

Spread batter into greased 13x9x2-inch baking pan. Decrease baking time to 30 minutes or until toothpick inserted comes out clean. Cook as directed. Cut into 24 bars.

Serves 24

Calories per serving:	134
Protein:	3 gm
Carbohydrate:	16 gm
Fat:	4 gm=27%

SUMMER TREAT

4 large	ripe bananas, peeled
1 pint	lemon sherbet
2 cups	strawberries, halved

1. Combine all ingredients in a blender or food processor. Blend until smooth.
2. Pour into glass and serve.

Serves 6

Calories per serving:	175
Protein:	2 gm
Carbohydrate:	41 gm
Fat:	2 gm=10%

FRUIT WHIRL

2	oranges or
1	grapefruit
2	apples, unpeeled
4	leaves of lettuce
4 tsp	unsweetened coconut, grated (optional)

1. Peel and separate oranges or grapefruit into segments.
2. Core unpeeled apples and slice into wedges.
3. Alternate citrus fruit and apple wedges on lettuce leaf to form a pinwheel. (Hint: Apples and oranges could be sliced crosswise in thin circles and alternated to form another colorful pattern.)
4. Sprinkle a small amount of grated coconut over fruit before serving.

Serves 4

Calories per serving:	84
Protein:	1 gm
Carbohydrate:	16 gm
Fat:	.5 gm=5%

HAZELNUT ANGEL FOOD CAKE

	non-stick cooking spray
1 cup	all-purpose flour, sifted
1/3 cup	super fine sugar
1/4 tsp	salt
1 1/2 cups	egg white (about 11 egg whites)
1 tsp	cream of tartar
3/4 cup	super fine sugar, divided
1 1/2 tsp	vanilla extract
1/4 cup	hazelnuts,finely ground, lightly toasted

1. Sift together flour, 1/3 cup sugar, and salt into a bowl; set aside.
2. Combine egg whites (at room temperature) and cream of tartar in a large bowl; beat until foamy. Gradually add 1/4 cup sugar, 1 Tbsp at a time, and beat until soft peaks form. Beat in vanilla.
3. Gently fold 1/3 of flour mixture into egg white mixture, adding 1/3 of mixture at a time. Fold in toasted hazelnuts in 2 portions. Fold in remaining 1/2 cup sugar in 3 portions. Spoon batter into a 10-inch tube pan coated with cooking spray.
4. Bake at 300° for 1 hour or until cake springs back when lightly touched. Remove from oven. Invert pan on funnel or bottle until cake is completely cooled (approximately 2 hours). Loosen cake from sides of pan, using a small metal spatula. Remove cake from pan, and slice with a serrated knife.

Serves 12

Calories per serving:	136
Protein:	4.4 gm
Carbohydrate:	26.2 gm
Fat:	1.6 gm=11%

FRUITY APPLE-RAISIN CRISP

3 med	firm cooking apples, peeled, cored, and sliced
1 Tbsp	lemon juice
1/2 cup	raisins
1/3 cup	firmly packed dark brown sugar
2 1/2 tsp	ground cinnamon
2 1/2 slices	whole wheat bread, crumbled
2 Tbsp	unsalted margarine

1. Preheat the oven to 300°. In a large bowl, toss the apples with the lemon juice, raisins, 1/4 cup brown sugar, and 1 1/2 tsp of the cinnamon. Spoon the mixture into an ungreased 9-inch pie pan and set aside.
2. To prepare the topping, spread the bread crumbs in a 15x10x1-inch jelly roll pan and bake, stirring occasionally, for 15 minutes or until dry. Remove the crumbs from the oven and transfer to a small bowl. In a small skillet or saucepan, melt the margarine over low heat. Add it to the crumbs along with the remaining 2 Tbsp brown sugar and the remaining 1 tsp cinnamon and mix well. Increase the oven temperature to 375°.
3. Sprinkle with crumb topping over the apples and bake for 30 minutes or until bubbly. (Note: If, after 10 minutes, the topping is browning too fast, cover loosely with aluminum foil.) Cool slightly before serving.

VARIATIONS:
Ginger-Peach Crisp—Prepare as directed, but substitute 4 cups sliced, peeled, and pitted peaches for the apples; omit the raisins, but add 3/4 tsp ground ginger.

Spoon the mixture into the pie pan and set aside. Instead of the topping called for, toss 1 1/2 cups gingersnap crumbs (about 3 gingersnaps) with 1 Tbsp dark brown sugar, 3/4 tsp ground ginger, and 2 Tbsp melted margarine. Sprinkle over the peaches and bake as directed.

Blueberry-Lemon Crisp—Prepare as directed, but substitute 4 cups blueberries for the apples and use golden raisins; omit the lemon juice and cinnamon and add 1 Tbsp grated lemon rind and 1 tsp ground nutmeg. Spoon the mixture into the pie pan and set aside. For the topping, substitute 1 1/2 cups melba toast crumbs tossed with 3 Tbsp dark brown sugar, 3/4 tsp grated lemon rind, 3/4 tsp ground nutmeg, and 2 Tbsp melted margarine. Sprinkle over the berries and bake as directed.

Serves 8

Calories per serving:	138
Protein:	1 gm
Carbohydrate:	28 gm
Fat:	3 gm=20%

TASTY LEMON SQUARES

	non-stick cooking spray
1 cup plus 4 1/2 tsp	all-purpose flour, sifted
1/3 cup plus 1 Tbsp	powdered sugar, sifted
1/2 tsp	baking powder
1/4 cup	cold unsalted margarine, cut into bits
2 Tbsp	ice water
1 large	egg
1 large	egg white
2/3 cup	granulated sugar
1/4 cup	lemon juice
1 tsp	lemon rind, grated
1/8 tsp	salt

1. Preheat the oven to 375°. Coat an 8x8x2-inch baking pan with the cooking spray and set aside.
2. In a medium-size mixing bowl, combine 1 cup flour, 1/3 cup powdered sugar, and 1/4 tsp of baking powder. Using a fork or pastry blender, cut in the margarine until the mixture resembles coarse meal. Sprinkle with the ice water and mix just until a small lump of dough pinched between the fingers holds together.
3. Pat the dough evenly over the bottom of the pan and bake for 20 minutes.
4. Meanwhile, in the small bowl of an electric mixer, beat the egg, egg white, granulated sugar, and lemon juice at moderate speed for 2 minutes or until the mixture is light and smooth. Whisk in the remaining 4 1/2 tsp flour, the lemon rind, the remaining 1/4 tsp baking powder, and the salt.

5. When the dough has finished baking, quickly remove the pan from the oven and pour the lemon mixture over it. Immediately return it to the oven, and bake for 25 minutes or until the lemon topping has set.
6. Place the pan upright in a wire rack and cool to room temperature—about 1 hour. Cut into squares and sift the remaining 1 Tbsp powdered sugar over the top before removing from the pan.

Makes 16 squares

Calories per serving:	103
Protein:	1 gm
Carbohydrate:	17 gm
Fat:	3 gm=26%

BLUEBERRY COBBLER

	non-stick cooking spray
1 1/2 cups	fresh blueberries, stemmed and sorted, or
1 1/2 cups	frozen dry-pack blueberries, thawed
1 Tbsp	orange-flavored liqueur, such as Cointreau (optional)
2 1/2 Tbsp	granulated sugar
2/3 cup	skim milk
1/3 cup	all-purpose flour, sifted
1 large	egg
1 tsp	orange rind, grated
2 tsp	vanilla extract
1/4 tsp	ground cinnamon
1 Tbsp	powdered sugar (optional)

1. Preheat the oven to 350°. Coat a 6-cup shallow baking dish with the cooking spray and set aside.
2. In a medium-size bowl, toss the blueberries with the orange-flavored liqueur, if desired, and 1 tsp of the granulated sugar, and let stand, uncovered, at room temperature for 30 minutes.
3. In a blender or food processor, combine 2 Tbsp of the granulated sugar and the milk, flour, egg, orange rind, vanilla extract, and cinnamon by whirling them for 5 seconds or until smooth.
4. Spoon the blueberries into the baking dish, pour the batter evenly over them, then sprinkle with the remaining 1 tsp granulated sugar.

5. Bake for 1 hour or until puffy and golden. Sprinkle with the powdered sugar, if desired, before serving.

Serves 4

Calories per serving:	137
Protein:	4 gm
Carbohydrate:	28 gm
Fat:	2 gm=13%

PEACH-BLUEBERRY TARTS

3 large	egg whites
1/8 tsp	salt
1/8 tsp	cream of tartar
3/4 cup	super fine sugar
1/2 tsp	vanilla extract
1 cup	fresh blueberries, stemmed and sorted, or
1 cup	frozen dry-packed blueberries, thawed
3 med	firm ripe peaches, peeled, pitted, and sliced
1 Tbsp	lemon juice
2 tsp	granulated sugar
1 tsp	lemon rind, grated

1. Preheat the oven to 250°. Line a baking sheet with baking parchment or waxed paper. Using a 3-inch biscuit cutter as a pattern, draw 6 3-inch circles about 2 inches apart in the parchment; set aside.
2. In a large bowl of an electric mixer, beat the egg whites and salt at moderate speed until foamy. Add the cream of tartar and beat until the whites hold soft peaks. Beat in the super fine sugar, 1 Tbsp at a time, then increase the speed to moderately high and continue to beat until the whites are glossy and hold peaks. Beat in the vanilla extract.
3. Fit a pastry bag with a 1/4-inch star tip, spoon in the egg whites, then pipe to fill in the circles on the parchment until about 1/3-inch thick. Pipe stars, just touching one another, around the edges to form borders 2 inches thick.
4. Bake the meringues for 1 hour, then turn off the oven and let them dry in the oven for 2-3 hours. (Note: The

meringues can be stored at this point.)

5. About 1 hour before serving, in a medium-size bowl, toss the peaches with the blueberries, lemon juice, granulated sugar, and lemon rind. Cover and refrigerate for 1 hour. Just before serving, spoon the fruit into the meringues, dividing the total amount evenly.

Note: The meringue shells may be stored in an air-tight container for about a week.

Serves 6

Calories per serving:	153
Protein:	2 gm
Carbohydrate:	37 gm
Fat:	Trace

LIME SOUFFLÉ

1/3 cup	granulated sugar
4 1/2 tsp	cornstarch
1/2 cup	skim milk
1 large	egg yolk
2 Tbsp	lime juice
1 tsp	lime rind, grated
1/2 tsp	vanilla extract
4 large	egg whites
1 Tbsp	powdered sugar (optional)

1. Preheat the oven to 350°. In a small heavy saucepan, combine the granulated sugar and cornstarch and slowly stir in the milk. Set over moderate heat and cook, stirring, until the mixture comes to a boil—about 2 minutes; cook, stirring, 30 seconds longer. Remove from the heat.

2. Mix 2 Tbsp of the hot milk mixture into the egg yolk, then stir the egg mixture back into the pan. Add the lime juice, lime rind, and vanilla extract, and mix thoroughly. Transfer to a medium-size heatproof bowl and cool to room temperature—about 1 hour—stirring occasionally to prevent a skin from forming on the surface.

3. In a large bowl, beat the egg whites at a moderately high speed until they hold soft peaks. With a rubber spatula, fold the whites into the cooled lime mixture. Spoon into a 1-quart soufflé or baking dish. Bake, uncovered, for 30-35 minutes or until the soufflé is puffy and lightly browned. Sift the powdered sugar on top, if desired, and serve immediately.

VARIATIONS:

Orange Soufflé—Prepare as directed, but substitute orange liqueur for the lime juice and 1 1/2 tsp grated orange rind for the lime rind. Omit the vanilla extract.

Lemon Soufflé—Prepare as directed, but substitute lemon juice for the lime juice and lemon rind for the lime rind.

Serves 6

Calories per serving:	78
Protein:	3 gm
Carbohydrate:	14 gm
Fat:	1 gm=12%

CHOCOLATE-RASPBERRY PARFAIT

2 cups	raspberries, fresh or frozen dry-pack, thawed
2 Tbsp	sugar or
1 packet	sugar substitute (or to taste)
2 cups	plain low fat yogurt
2 Tbsp	cocoa powder (not a mix)
4 tsp	wheat germ
4 sprigs	mint (optional)

1. In a medium-size bowl, combine the raspberries with 1 Tbsp of the sugar and set aside.
2. In another medium-size bowl, combine yogurt, cocoa powder, and remaining 1 Tbsp sugar, whisking until smooth and creamy.
3. Spoon 1/4 cup of the yogurt mixture into each of 4 8-ounce parfait glasses; top with 1/4 cup of the raspberries; then sprinkle with 1/2 tsp of the wheat germ. Make 3 more layers, ending with the yogurt. Refrigerate for 2-3 hours before serving. Garnish, if you like, with mint.

Serves 4

Calories per serving:	106
Protein:	5 gm
Carbohydrate:	20 gm
Fat:	2 gm=17%

ANGEL FOOD CAKE WITH CHOCOLATE GLAZE

1 3/4 cups	egg whites (about 12 eggs)
1 1/2 tsp	cream of tartar
1/4 tsp	salt
1 1/2 cups	granulated sugar
1 1/4 cups	cake flour, sifted
2 tsp	vanilla extract
3/4 tsp	almond extract
3/4 tsp	fresh lemon juice

1. In large mixing bowl, combine egg whites, cream of tartar, and salt. Beat egg whites just to very soft peak. Turn mixer to lowest speed and gradually add sugar, 1 Tbsp at a time.
2. Keep mixer on lowest speed, add flour, 1 Tbsp at a time. Do not overmix. Fold in vanilla, almond extract, and lemon juice.
3. Using a spatula, transfer the batter to a non-stick angel food cake pan. Run the spatula down deep through the batter to break any air pockets. Bake on bottom rack of a 350° oven 45-50 minutes or until cake is golden and cracks on top feel dry.
4. Invert pan and let cool. Remove from pan onto serving platter.

Serves 12

Calories per serving:	148
Protein:	4 gm
Carbohydrate:	33 gm
Fat:	Trace

CHOCOLATE GLAZE

1 cup	powdered sugar, sifted
2 Tbsp	non-fat milk, cold
1 tsp	unsweetened cocoa powder

1. In a small bowl, combine powdered sugar and milk. Stir until smooth.
2. Add cocoa powder and stir until smooth.

Frosts one cake

Calories per serving:	51
Protein:	Trace
Carbohydrate:	13 gm
Fat:	Trace

RASPBERRY DELIGHT

5	egg whites
1/2 tsp	cream of tartar
2 tsp	vanilla extract
2/3 cup	granulated sugar
1/2 cup	low fat vanilla yogurt
10 oz	frozen raspberries in heavy syrup, thawed

1. In a bowl, beat egg whites until foamy; add cream of tartar and vanilla. Beat 1 minute.
2. Gradually add sugar, 1 Tbsp at a time, and beat until egg whites form stiff peaks.
3. Line a 10-inch round pizza pan with a paper lunch bag trimmed to pan size. Spread mixture evenly over covered baking sheet to form a circle. Use a spoon to smooth center and edges. (A cookie sheet may be used in place of a pizza pan but spread mixture to form a circle.) Bake in a 275° oven for 1 hour. Cool on wire rack for 1 hour.
4. Remove to serving plate. Spread vanilla yogurt over meringue. Top with berries. Serve at once.

Serves 6

Calories per serving:	145
Protein:	4 gm
Carbohydrate:	29 gm
Fat:	Trace

LEMON ICE CREAM

1/3 cup	fresh lemon juice
1 1/2 tsp	lemon peel
1 1/3 cups	evaporated skim milk
1	egg
1 1/2 cups	granulated sugar
3/4 cup	cold non-fat milk

1. Combine and refrigerate lemon juice and lemon peel.
2. Pour evaporated milk into a mixing bowl. Chill in freezer until ice crystals form around edges, about 1 1/2 hours or shorter if milk is already cold. (Chill beater blades also.)
3. Beat chilled milk with egg on high speed until it is the consistency of heavy cream, about 5 minutes. Gradually add sugar and beat until mixture thickens.
4. Add lemon juice and lemon zest; beat 2 minutes.
5. Add cold non-fat milk and beat 1 minute more.
6. Pour into ice cream freezer and process according to manufacturer's directions.
7. Scoop into stemmed glasses. Top with blueberries or raspberries, if desired.

Serves 4

Calories per serving:	127
Protein:	3 gm
Carbohydrate:	29 gm
Fat:	Trace

LEMON LIFT

2 cups	fresh lemon ice cream
10 oz	low-calorie natural cherry seltzer or mineral water
4	strawberries
4	sprigs of fresh mint

1. Combine the ice cream and seltzer and mix well or blend until smooth.
2. Garnish with sliced strawberries and a sprig of fresh mint.

Serves 4

Calories per serving:	131
Protein:	3 gm
Carbohydrate:	31 gm
Fat:	Trace

LADYFINGERS

3	whole eggs, separated
2	egg whites
2/3 cup	granulated sugar
1 tsp	vanilla extract
3/4 cup	all-purpose flour, plus 1 Tbsp
1/4 tsp	safflower margarine (in a tub)
1 tsp	cornmeal
	powdered sugar (optional)

1. In a large bowl of an electric mixer, beat egg whites to soft peaks; gradually beat in 1/3 cup of the sugar and beat until stiff peaks form.
2. In a small bowl, whisk egg yolks until thick and lemon colored. Whisk in vanilla. Fold into egg white.
3. In a flour sifter, combine remaining 1/3 cup sugar with flour. Sift into egg mixture and carefully fold.
4. Grease ladyfinger pans or small muffin tins with margarine. Sprinkle with cornmeal. Spoon batter into pans until each section or cup is about 2/3 full.
5. Bake at 375° 12 minutes or until browned. Cool on racks. If desired, sprinkle with powdered sugar.

Serves 3 dozen

Calories per serving:	31
Protein:	1 gm
Carbohydrate:	6 gm
Fat:	Trace

STRAWBERRY COBBLER

3/4 cup	water
2 Tbsp	cornstarch
1/2 cup	granulated sugar
3 cups	strawberries

Topping:

1 cup	all-purpose flour, sifted
1/2 tsp	salt
1 1/2 tsp	baking powder
1/3 cup	non-fat milk
3 Tbsp	safflower oil

1. In a medium saucepan, combine water, cornstarch, and sugar, and bring to a boil. Cook 1 minute, stirring constantly. Add berries and remove from heat. Pour into a 9- or 10-inch pie plate.
2. Combine flour, salt, and baking powder. Mix milk with oil and add to flour. Using a fork or pastry blender, work dough into a ball. Drop by spoonfuls onto fruit cobbler.
3. Bake at 415° 25-30 minutes or until topping is lightly browned.

Serves 8

Calories per serving:	172
Protein:	2 gm
Carbohydrate:	29 gm
Fat:	5 gm=26%

ANGEL PUDDING CAKE

1	vanilla angel food cake
3/4 cup	orange juice, freshly squeezed
1 Tbsp	gelatin
1/4 cup	all-purpose flour
2/3 cup	granulated sugar, plus 3 Tbsp
1/4 tsp	salt
2 cups	skim milk
3	eggs, separated
1 Tbsp	grated orange peel

1. Prepare the cake according to instructions.
2. Combine orange juice and gelatin; set aside.
3. In a double boiler over boiling water, combine flour, 2/3 cup of the sugar, salt, and milk. Cook and stir until thickened, about 10 minutes.
4. Stir in gelatin, egg yolks, and orange peel. Remove from heat at once and cool.
5. Cut cooked cake into bite-size pieces.
6. Beat egg whites to soft peaks. Add the remaining 3 Tbsp sugar and beat 2-3 minutes. Fold into custard.
7. Alternate layers of cake and custard in a non-stick bundt pan. Refrigerate at least 6 hours.

Serves 12

Calories per serving:	245
Protein:	8 gm
Carbohydrate:	51 gm
Fat:	1 gm=4%

MELON ROUNDS

1/2	cantaloupe, peeled, seeded, and cut crosswise into rounds 1-inch thick
1 1/2 cups	fresh raspberries
1/2	lime, cut into wedges

1. Arrange melon rounds on chilled dessert plates. Fill with berries. Garnish with lime wedges.

Serves 4

Calories per serving:	28
Protein:	Trace
Carbohydrate:	7 gm
Fat:	Trace

AMARETTO ORANGES

3 large	navel oranges, peeled, sliced into thin rings, and then torn or cut into sections
2 Tbsp	amaretto liqueur
6	strawberries, thinly sliced
4 whole	strawberries or maraschino cherries

1. Arrange oranges in a shallow bowl; pour amaretto over oranges and toss. Chill 2 hours or overnight.
2. Just before serving, line the edges of 4 small dessert plates with sliced strawberries. Arrange orange sections in center. Top with whole strawberries or cherries.

Serves 4

Calories per serving:	71
Protein:	1 gm
Carbohydrate:	16 gm
Fat:	Trace

ANISETTE CANTALOUPE

1/2	cantaloupe
7 Tbsp	anisette liqueur
3 1/2 Tbsp	water
1/4	watermelon
	sprigs of fresh mint

1. Using a melon baller, form balls from cantaloupe. Combine 3 Tbsp of the anisette with 1 1/2 Tbsp of the water; pour over cantaloupe balls. Cover and chill 1-2 hours.
2. Remove rind from watermelon. Cut melon into wedges. Combine remaining 4 Tbsp anisette with remaining 2 Tbsp water; pour over melon. Chill 1-2 hours.
3. To serve, arrange watermelon triangles symmetrically on chilled individual dessert plates.
4. Top each triangle with a melon ball. Garnish with remaining melon balls and mint.

Serves 6

Calories per serving:	117
Protein:	1 gm
Carbohydrate:	19 gm
Fat:	Trace

KIWI ICE

4	kiwi, peeled and cubed
2 cups	unsweetened apple juice
1 Tbsp	lemon juice
1/2 tsp	grated orange rind
	orange slices

1. Combine fruit juices in a blender and process until smooth. Stir in orange rind.
2. Pour mixture into an 8-inch square baking pan. Freeze until almost firm.
3. Spoon frozen mixture into a mixing bowl. Beat with an electric mixer until fluffy. Return to pan and freeze until firm.
4. Let stand at room temperature 10 minutes before serving. Garnish with orange slices.

Serves 4

Calories per serving:	26
Protein:	0.3 gm
Carbohydrate:	6.1 gm
Fat:	0.2 gm=7%

PEACH DELIGHT

1/2 cup	sugar
1 cup	water
3 cups	peaches, peeled and sliced (about 4 large, ripe peaches)
2 Tbsp	lemon or lime juice

1. In a small heavy saucepan, combine the sugar and water and cook over low heat, uncovered, for 5 minutes or until the sugar dissolves. Cool for 30 minutes; refrigerate, covered, for 4 hours.
2. In a blender or food processor, whirl the peaches for 1 minute. Add the syrup and lemon juice and whirl for 30 seconds or until blended.
3. Freeze in an ice cream freezer following manufacturer's directions, then proceed to step 5, or freeze in a 13x9x2-inch pan until firm—about 3 hours.
4. Remove the pan from the freezer. Break the ice into chunks and transfer to the large bowl of an electric mixer. Beat at high speed until light and fluffy.
5. Spoon into a 1/2-gallon freezer container, cover, and freeze at least 4 hours before serving.

Serves 12

Calories per serving:	51
Protein:	0 gm
Carbohydrate:	13 gm
Fat:	0 gm

FRESH FRUIT TOPPING

2 cups	fresh fruit: strawberries, raspberries, peaches, or other fruit
2 Tbsp	cornstarch
1/2 cup	water

1. Chop fruit into large pieces.
2. Whisk cornstarch into cool water and bring to a boil.
3. Add 1 cup fruit and bring to a boil again.
4. Immediately remove from heat and add remaining fruit. Leave last cup of fruit uncooked. Serve hot or cold.

Serves 8

Calories per serving:	20
Protein:	Trace
Carbohydrate:	5 gm
Fat:	Trace

CINNAMON SPREAD

1 cup	low fat cottage cheese
1 tsp	lemon juice
2 Tbsp	skim milk
1 tsp	cinnamon
1 Tbsp	sugar

1. Blend all ingredients together until creamy.
2. Chill before serving.

Serves 4

Calories per serving:	10
Protein:	1 gm
Carbohydrate:	2 gm
Fat:	Trace

Index